D0946436

DATE DUE

MAY 0 8 2009

LYNNFIELD PUBLIC LIBRARY
LYNNFIELD, MASS. 01940

JOURNEY OUT OF DARKNESS

Praeger Security International Advisory Board

Board Cochairs

Loch K. Johnson, Regents Professor of Public and International Affairs, School of Public and International Affairs, University of Georgia (U.S.A.)

Paul Wilkinson, Professor of International Relations and Chairman of the Advisory Board, Centre for the Study of Terrorism and Political Violence, University of St. Andrews (U.K.)

Members

Anthony H. Cordesman, Arleigh A. Burke Chair in Strategy, Center for Strategic and International Studies (U.S.A.)

Thérèse Delpech, Director of Strategic Affairs, Atomic Energy Commission, and Senior Research Fellow, CERI (Fondation Nationale des Sciences Politiques), Paris (France)

Sir Michael Howard, former Chichele Professor of the History of War and Regis Professor of Modern History, Oxford University, and Robert A. Lovett Professor of Military and Naval History, Yale University (U.K.)

Lieutenant General Claudia J. Kennedy, USA (Ret.), former Deputy Chief of Staff for Intelligence, Department of the Army (U.S.A.)

Paul M. Kennedy, J. Richardson Dilworth Professor of History and Director, International Security Studies, Yale University (U.S.A.)

Robert J. O'Neill, former Chichele Professor of the History of War, All Souls College, Oxford University (Australia)

Shibley Telhami, Anwar Sadat Chair for Peace and Development, Department of Government and Politics, University of Maryland (U.S.A.)

Fareed Zakaria, Editor, Newsweek International (U.S.A.)

JOURNEY OUT OF DARKNESS

The Real Story of American Heroes in
Hitler's POW Camps

An Oral History

Hal LaCroix

Photographs by Jorg Meyer

PRAEGER SECURITY INTERNATIONAL
Westport, Connecticut • London

LYNNFIELD PUBLIC LIBRARY
LYNNFIELD, MASS. 01940

Library of Congress Cataloging-in-Publication Data

LaCroix, Hal, 1960–
   Journey out of darkness : the real story of American heroes in Hitler's POW camps :
   an oral history / Hal LaCroix; photographs by Jorg Meyer
      p. cm.
   Includes bibliographical references and index.
   ISBN-13: 978–0–275–99744–1 (alk. paper)

1. World War, 1939–1945—Prisoners and prisons, German. 2. World War, 1939–1945—
Personal narratives, American. 3. Prisoners of war—Germany—Biography. 4. Prisoners of
war—United States—Biography. 5. Ex-concentration camp inmates—United States—
Biography. 6. Veterans—United States—Biography. 7. Oral history. I. Meyer, Jorg,
1968- II. Title.
D805.G3L237 2007
940.54'7243092273—dc22   2007016135

British Library Cataloguing in Publication Data is available.

Copyright © 2007 by Hal LaCroix and Jorg Meyer

All rights reserved. No portion of this book may be
reproduced, by any process or technique, without the
express written consent of the publisher.

Library of Congress Catalog Card Number: 2007016135
ISBN-13: 978–0–275–99744–1

First published in 2007

Praeger Security International, 88 Post Road West, Westport, CT 06881
An imprint of Greenwood Publishing Group, Inc.
www.praeger.com

Printed in the United States of America

The paper used in this book complies with the
Permanent Paper Standard issued by the National
Information Standards Organization (Z39.48–1984).

10 9 8 7 6 5 4 3 2 1

4-4-08

To the wives and families.—HL

To my three daughters: Jule, Gretchen, and Paulina.—JM

"In the truest sense, freedom cannot be bestowed; it must be achieved."

Franklin Delano Roosevelt

CONTENTS

INTRODUCTION

How can we possibly understand what they have endured?

Sympathy is our first reaction, ideally followed by gratitude for sacrifice. Perhaps on Memorial and Veterans Days we visit the stone monuments and listen to the bugle's call. Nervously we follow the news about today's soldiers fighting and dying in distant lands. We wish our boys home, soon. And yet, unless we have suffered in similar circumstances, it is hard to understand what a soldier at war has endured.

In the United States, attitudes about returning soldiers have varied considerably during the past century. On one end of the spectrum are veterans of the Vietnam War, who often faced disdain and accusation from a nation divided by a controversial war. World War I veterans were celebrated for tipping the balance on European battlefields, even as they came home to spread a strain of influenza that killed millions of Americans. Vets returning in recent years from Iraq and Afghanistan, while treated with due respect and honor, encounter a country that to a large degree is disengaged from those wars.

It is for the veterans of World War II—aged men congregated in coffee shops, puttering in their yards, holed up in condos and rest homes—that we have reserved our fondest, least complicated tributes. They fought the Good War, after all, emerging triumphant against evil—and let us not dwell for too long on the chaos and carnage.

How, though, do we perceive soldiers who suffered as prisoners of war? How do we react to those men who disappeared into the enemy's world, like ghosts, who were overcome (a little too easily, say the whispers) and herded away to "sit out the war" safely behind wire? How can we know them?

The answer, surely, is one by one. Story by story, face by face, and man by man. From singular encounters emerges a larger picture, both startling and moving, of American soldiers and airmen held prisoner by enemy forces. The POWs of WW II featured in this book—and by extension the POWs of every war—deserve special attention because they fought a double war, in combat and captivity, each war delivering a separate and lasting shock to the system.

Twelve of the POWs in *Journey Out of Darkness* were infantrymen (including one paratrooper) captured between the June 1944 D-Day landings and the conflagration that was the Battle of the Bulge in December 1944; a thirteenth grunt was captured earlier in 1944 during fighting near Anzio, Italy. Five other POWs profiled here, airmen, had the pleasure of diving from burning planes into Nazi Germany.

We have included a nineteenth man, a Navy submariner named Gabe Paiva, in order to honor those captured in the Pacific Theater. Suffering profoundly as a POW in the Philippines and Japan, Gabe found strength where no strength should remain. Equally remarkable, even heroic, has been his ability to forgive his captors.

All but three of these POWs were citizen soldiers who were drafted or enlisted themselves after the attack on Pearl Harbor. By and large they were first- or second-generation immigrant kids of European descent raised in poor households during the Great Depression. Their combat experiences were hazardous and horrifying. But unlike other surviving servicemen, they were ushered into a second, grueling struggle marked by depravation and a shattering loss of control.

More often than not, this second war has eclipsed the first in the minds and hearts of the men, and in the estimation of their countrymen. Former POWs have commonly encountered not acclaim for their combat exploits, or admiration for surviving the camps, but ambivalence or disdain. (Here, perhaps, the experiences of POWs from WW II and Vietnam vets converge.) The military was actively complicit, instructing repatriated men not to talk about their captivity.

The former POWs featured here, by and large, did not open up about their wartime experiences until their retirements, when they met each other in POW support groups run by the Department of Veterans Affairs in Massachusetts.

Although less than 3 percent of American POWs perished inside Nazi Germany—a figure not counting the hundreds of fliers who were murdered or died of wounds shortly after parachuting to earth—captivity left its survivors with chronic and debilitating physical problems, as well as searing emotional and psychological damage. And now they are dying off: of the roughly 100,000–120,000 American POWs held captive in German-occupied lands (the number is in considerable dispute), less than 16,000 survive today, and several more die each day. Four of the 19 men in this book have died since they were first contacted by the authors in 2004.

The POWs of WW II are fading away, but there is another reason for taking a clearer look at their experiences: the story, as most people know it, is simply wrong.

Movies such as *The Great Escape* and TV shows like *Hogan's Heroes* have shaped public consciousness in ways that are profoundly misleading. These entertainments depict POWs in Germany as healthy enough, milling about in adequate clothing and treated with relative decency by captors ascribing to the Geneva Convention. Invariably, Hollywood POWs are wisecracking con men bravely hatching escape and sabotage plans that, of course, succeed or at least show up the hapless Germans. Our guys fulfill the ideal of American ingenuity and daring.

POWs displayed bravery and ingenuity, indeed, but of a very different sort. The popularized depiction is at best removed from the truth, at worst an unjust fabrication. Admittedly, *Hogan's Heroes* was slapstick comedy, so campy that few viewers could have seen it as realistic. Nonetheless, in the absence of more realistic stories, such breezy adventure tales helped form a lasting perception of the Hearty American and the Good (if bumbling) German.

Hollywood followed the government line that American POWs were badly mistreated *only* by the Japanese (a message that reflected the bloodthirsty and racist nature of the Pacific War). The Allies were committed to enlisting the German state in the coming struggle against the Soviets; images of emaciated POWs and tales of cruel oppression, certainly, would not bolster support for that effort. Germans brutalized Jews, the postwar narrative proclaimed. Japanese brutalized Americans.

The movie *King Rat,* about Allied POWs in Japan, actually defined itself against the situation in Germany. Its preamble states: "The inmates of Changi had no friendly Swiss border or any other neutral country within reach." As if the Swiss somehow exercised influence over the Nazis; as if it were just a hop, skip, and a jump to the land of chocolate once a POW slipped the wire.

Yes, the Japanese treated their POWs abominably. Four out of 10 Allied prisoners died in captivity in the Pacific, primarily from tropical diseases, beheadings, beatings, and starvation. Thousands were worked to death as slave labor for now-thriving companies such as Kawasaki and Nippon. In comparison, the suffering of American POWs in Germany could be considered bearable. And, of course, nearly any example of group suffering pales next to the overarching evil that was the Holocaust.

But one form of suffering does not eliminate another. The heroic endurance of American POWs in Europe should be truthfully honored, and the truth is that in the bowels of the Nazi war machine they fought an unrelenting battle against brutality, dysentery, loneliness, and overwork. They fought it without decent medical care or warm clothing. They fought it not knowing if they would be lined up the next day and shot as Hitler's revenge.

And they starved. A typical POW lost one-third to one-half of his body weight, and many resembled survivors of the Holocaust by the spring of 1945. Six more months of war, it can reasonably be asserted, would have seen tens of thousands of Allied POWs starve to death.

POWs largely disappeared from view. Mail tended to be infrequent or nonexistent. Red Cross packages were scarce, routinely stolen by the Nazis or German civilians. It was not uncommon for POW families in the United States to go several months and even years before learning that their loved ones had not perished but were alive inside the Thousand Year Reich. In fact, more than a few liberated POWs nearly beat home telegrams carrying news of their capture.

In the movies, POWs tunnel like moles. In reality, escape for most POWs was a pipe dream. The men were too exhausted from hunger and labor, the camps were securely maintained, and their German guards were not, in fact, farcical idiots. Some guards acted brutally, some displayed kindness, and most simply followed orders.

The tentacles of anti-Semitism extended to POWs in Germany. If you were a Jewish POW—as were two of the men in this book—you were likely to be segregated, starved more aggressively, and in some cases worked to death. Many Jewish POWs realized this and concealed their religious background; some knew what awaited them and nonetheless refused to hide their heritage.

In addition, tens of thousands of POWs suffered greatly during the war's final winter when they were force-marched away from advancing Russian troops. POWs lucky enough to be liberated by the Russians were rarely given transport to Allied lines but abandoned to journey hundreds of miles on their own across war-ravaged lands to the port of Odessa.

The real story of American POWs in Germany is far grimmer than the Hollywood concoction, but also more surprising and fascinating—in the end, more inspiring—than any prison camp movie or stalag sitcom. The experiences of the 19 men in this book coalesce to reveal universal truths about the human condition under the stress of captivity in wartime.

Readers will learn, first and foremost, that a central experience of American POWs held in Nazi Germany is their struggle with feelings of guilt, shame, and overwhelming regret—both during and after the war. (The former POWs profiled here have benefited from counseling provided by the Department of Veterans Affairs, and therefore are not entirely representative. We can only speculate about those who died in the decades after the war—from illness, alcoholism, suicide, or other causes—or who endure today but have not "come in from the cold.") Former POWs can be haunted men, forever asking "Why me?" and besieged by silent implications of cowardice.

Despite this unwarranted sense of shame, POWs also showed a remarkable ability to accept their meager circumstances and make necessary adaptations for survival. Adjusting for the lack of personal control and privacy—worse than Army life, which could be humiliating enough—was a difficult challenge for independent-minded Americans who, at the same time, clung to the hope of liberation. It is heartening, against this backdrop, to hear stories of kindness, friendship, and love played out in the camps. These qualities endured, against all odds.

Some POWs, sadly, recoiled at their circumscribed worlds and spiraled down into themselves. Captivity could prompt spiritual crisis and a loss of faith in God. Many POWs emerged from their ordeals both alienated and traumatized, and often in denial that they had a problem. For these men the shadows of imprisonment have been long, their journeys into the light wrenching.

The real story of Americans in Hitler's POW camps, ultimately, provokes hard questions about courage and heroism. What is a hero? Does it take a special brand of courage just to endure, to survive?

It is intended that the photographs and stories of *Journey Out of Darkness* work together to create an authentic appreciation of the POW experience in Nazi Germany. But it does not end there, unfortunately. Through these old men we begin to know the young men who fight today's wars and are returning, one by one, into our midst. We glimpse the struggles they will face many years from now when they, too, are old and fading from our memories.

CHAPTER 1

The Pull of the Past

I AM NOT A KILLER: MARCEL BOISVERT'S STORY

He understands, actually, the feelings of the German civilians who wanted to tear apart the American and English *terrorfliegers* who floated to earth from their wounded machines, the men who had bombed their homes and brewed hellish, flesh-consuming fire storms in their cities. He probably would have felt the same way, he admits, if the roles had been reversed.

"You never let anyone know you're a flier or they'll string you up," states Marcel Boisvert, forced to bail out on his fourth mission over Germany, to parachute down a corridor of "unbelievable silence," and knowing as he dropped the stories of airmen killed by mobs below. He is 80 years old now, then 18. "Keep you head down," he says. "Keep your mouth shut."

Marcel was a tail gunner on a B-17, the bomber dubbed the Queen of the Sky. For the tail gunner, packed backwards into a glassed-in cage at the rear of the plane, the world was always in retreat. Gripping twin 50s and straddling a bicycle seat, Marcel's job was to fire at German fighter planes appearing with sudden vengeance from the going-away world (none showed on his brief watch). Shells hurled from 25,000 feet below exploded into black and white smudges all around him. Flak scraped along the belly of the plane like kicked-up gravel. To this day, Marcel cannot stand to watch fireworks; he has seen enough. And he never sits backwards on a moving train.

On his first three missions, they bombed railroad marshalling yards and power plants. The first and third sorties were "milk runs," easy. On the second mission, the engines were hit and pilot Dean Anderson (tall and blond,

Marcel Boisvert

says Marcel, the Big-Man-on-Campus type) coaxed the plane to an emergency field in France. According to standard procedure, Marcel stayed in the tail during the tough landing. Their fourth mission targeted Dresden, called *Elbeflorenz* or "Florence on the Elbe River."

    Dresden, renowned for its opera, art, and delicate china, was flooded with war wounded and refugees fleeing the Red Army. On February 13, 1945, Allied planes dropped 3,907 tons of bombs and incendiary devices on the city, killing between 50,000 and 100,000 people. Over 25,000 homes were destroyed. More people died in Dresden, some believe, than perished in Hiroshima. Experts argue about the totals. For days afterward, bonfires of bodies lit the night sky.

"It was a mission," says Marcel, flatly. Airmen flew missions.

On the return leg from Dresden, a shell exploded so close to the plane that it flipped over and spiraled down. The pilot hit the bailout switch; alarm bells clanged; the crew scrambled to get out. The first four men to jump, including Marcel, came down over enemy lines and were immediately captured by German soldiers. The next five, including the golden-boy pilot, caught a favorable wind and fell into the arms of American forces in France. So much for getting out first. The lucky ones were given leave in Paris; the captured ones sloughed into the Nazi Fatherland. Marcel's shoes were snatched by civilians and then he was shipped to an interrogation center outside Frankfurt and thrown into an 8-by-10-foot cell.

A board for a bed, no mattress. A tiny window leaking light, beyond his reach. A bucket toilet and one coffee can of cabbage soup per day. Lines counting time scraped into the wall. Marcel, the child of a house storming with seven brothers and sisters, sat in isolation for two days. But he did not despair. "I was defiant," he says. "I was a cocky little bastard."

They took him to an interrogation room. A German officer sat at a table. Another stood, and two guards took their places behind Marcel. The questions started about his bomber group and the tactics of strategic area bombing. He shot back: name, rank, serial number; name, rank, serial number; again and again. Hours went by. The officer at the table, always polite, told him in excellent English: "We've got you listed as a spy, we'll shoot you." Then they brought him back to his cell and days passed in exactly the same manner as before. Two days, maybe three. The guards came again.

This time the polite officer asked Marcel, with a worried tone in his voice: "Did you go to Dresden? I had family in Dresden."

Did he go to Dresden? Marcel thought so, that had been the mission objective. But sometimes planes were diverted or lost their way. They could have dropped their load on a secondary target or a "target of opportunity." A tail gunner did not really know what happened in the cockpit. He lived backwards in a world of deadly fireworks, of fighter planes lurking in clouds, of sky slipping away. But yes, that was the target at the daily briefing, Dresden.

"I don't know," Marcel replied.

Strangely, his interrogators already knew the name of his bomber group, that he was a tail gunner, even his hometown of Dover, New Hampshire. Marcel is not sure how they knew, maybe from American newspaper clippings. "We can't learn anything from you," one of the officers scoffed. But he was a spy, nonetheless, and they took Marcel outside and showed him

Here Marcel Boisvert is dressed as a typical European in his "escape photo." The photos, carried by bomber crewmen in case they were shot down and eluded capture behind enemy lines, were to be used in forged documents provided by the underground. Every flier wore this same tie in his photo, laughs Marcel.

three tall posts in the ground. "This," said the polite officer, "is where you're going to be shot tomorrow." Then they threw him back in his cell.

"I didn't know what the hell to think," says Marcel. A day passed. And another. Six or seven days dissolved in the cell, trailed like smoke out the tiny window beyond his reach, and then the guards took him again. To the posts, to his end? They put him in a truck bound for a POW distribution camp.

Marcel sits now in a sun room carpeted with artificial turf, overlooking his swimming pool. He is surrounded by toys for grandchildren, including an old-fashioned hobby horse on springs. A retired orthodontist, he lives in a beautiful house in the suburbs with an American flag out front and a digital TV dish jutting off the garage. The yard is in full summer bloom. Marcel, though, cannot care for it anymore because of the arthritis in his hands. The shiny sedan in the driveway carries a license plate outlined in barbed wire, identifying him as a former POW.

He is a big believer in self-reliance, boasting that his three children are hard workers all. They are college graduates, too, he adds, and they have given Marcel eight grandchildren with more, he hopes, on the way. The clothesline by the pool is pegged with the kids' dried-out swim trunks. Marcel's life is the American dream.

His dad, a French Canadian immigrant, dug sewer trenches for the Work Projects Administration during the Depression. The family was on and off welfare. Marcel helped by selling the *Concord Monitor* on the street and caddying at a private golf club, where he made 25 cents a day and gave it to his mother for food. It never occurred to him that he would play golf himself. "That was out of our class," he says. (He did learn to play decades later, but insisted on making his own clubs.)

Because Marcel's folks could not afford to buy him a bicycle, he built one from parts he scrounged at the dump. Only his bike did not have brakes, so he disembarked by riding into trees or just bailing out. Then he would pick himself up—foolish, yes, but always persistent. That's how he snared an after-school job at a First National grocery store, by going back seven, eight times to ask for it.

Persistent, yes, but not particularly ambitious. Marcel was an average student and figured he would be a laborer, like his old man. "I was strong willed, a typical teenager," he says, and he did not bother reading the newspaper, preferring radio shows like *The Lone Ranger* and *The Invisible Man*. But when he heard about the attack on Pearl Harbor during a Sea Scout expedition, the news shocked him out of his bubble. (Like many Americans, he had never heard of the Navy base.) Turning 18 the following September, Marcel volunteered for the Army Air Corps. He wanted to be a bombardier —"Bomb the bastards," he said during his psychological test—and that was a bit strange, he was told, not wanting to be a pilot like everyone else.

At his first POW camp for officers, a Dulag Luft, Marcel received a pair of shoes three sizes too big for his feet. The barracks were raised on stilts and vicious dogs roamed the camp at night. Through a dirty window, by moonlight, he watched B-17s bomb the village of Wetzler where optical devices and bomb sites were said to be manufactured. Back home his parents watched the mail, first receiving a telegram listing their son as wounded, followed soon after by a second telegram listing him as missing, followed weeks later by yet another telegram confirming his capture.

In the meantime, Marcel was sent by train—75 POWs crammed in a "40-by-8" boxcar made for 40 men and 8 horses—and it was awful, suffocating. The men suffered with dysentery. A single bucket for a toilet overflowed. The train, moving only at night, took three or four days to arrive at Stalag 13D.

"I didn't trust anyone there," Marcel says. He resisted making buddies and refused to eat the black bread. "I built a shield." Years later, in the

Marcel Boisvert as a young soldier.

1980s, a psychologist with the Veterans Administration said that was the worst thing he could have done. Fortunately, a POW captured years earlier in North Africa counseled Marcel to take better care of himself. Keep your socks dry, the man advised, eat what they give you. Do what it takes to survive. The cocky kid listened for once. His weight loss slowed.

Months passed and Marcel had to accept help again. In the chaos of April 1945, he took part in a grueling forced march from Stalag 13D to the POW camp at Moosburg. His feet became bloated and infected, but he did not want to step from the column because severely wounded men, rumor had it, were being shot by the Germans. When he could no longer walk, Marcel climbed into a cart pulled by fellow POWs and depended on them to get him there alive.

After the war—just as before it—Marcel was not sure what to do. He gorged himself on his mother's cooking, and by night she sat by his bed as he thrashed with nightmares, as he jumped over and over from the spiraling plane on its Dresden run, but this time his chute would not open and he fell endlessly through the column of unbelievable silence. Marcel's mother never

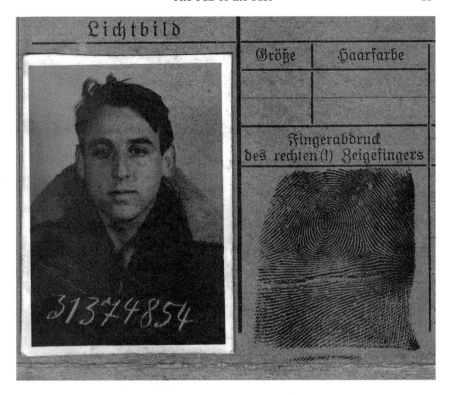

Lichtbild

Größe | Haarfarbe

Fingerabbruck
des rechten (!) Zeigefingers

31374854

This photograph of Marcel Boisvert, pasted into a German document next to his
thumbprint, was taken roughly two weeks after the sleep-deprived flier's capture.

said a word about it; he did not learn about her vigil until his sister told him
many years later.

Confused or not, it was against his constitution to loiter. Marcel took
"gut work" on the railroad, earning 63 cents a day, then reenlisted in the
Army ("What else did I know?") only to find himself disgusted and forlorn
running a motor pool in Guam. So it was back home to Dover where,
against the superintendent's advice, he enrolled for a year of academic
courses at the high school. "Best decision I ever made," Marcel says.
("You're an old man!" one amazed kid informed him in science class.)

Something clicked. The nightmares started to fade and things "relaxed
inside" a little bit. He attended the University of New Hampshire and then
was accepted at Tufts University Dental School. "You'll be out in six
months and earning a living," his father commented. At Marcel's graduation four years later, the old man admitted, "If I wasn't here today, I
wouldn't believe it."

Marcel Boisvert

The decades rolled away, as they do, and his POW memories burrowed beneath life's joys and struggles. Marcel and his wife Barbara had three children—with relish he calls her an "aggressive Irishwoman;" she nags him for not being happy, not smiling enough—and he studied at night to become an orthodontist. He kept busy, busy, busy, mind and body, and he rarely talked about being a POW—but *not*, Marcel firmly asserts, not because he thought he was a coward. He just saw no advantage in discussing it. It made things awkward, brought up too many bad memories. Life went on.

The German officer's question, though, did not entirely disappear. Every now and then it sounded in his mind, softly. "Did you go to Dresden?" the man asked. He *had* family in Dresden. "Did you go to Dresden?"

The officer asked the question for 40 years. Then in 1985, at a convention of his bomber group, Marcel learned something remarkable. A fellow airman showed him official records proving that Marcel's plane did not, in fact, go to Dresden. It had been diverted to Brux, Czechoslovakia, to attack a synthetic oil plant, a military target. No one had told Marcel in the tail of the plane.

"I was glad to hear it," he says. "I am not a killer."

But he knows, of course, that he could have gone to Dresden. That he did not, in the end, had nothing to do with him. He was just another airman, hoping against all odds to survive enough missions to go home. One more tail gunner among thousands of tail gunners, flying backwards over Europe, primed and ready to protect his crew mates in the front of the plane. He was just another airman: hero to the gang back home, *terrorflieger* to the people below, expendable to the military machine. He could have gone to Dresden.

"War is like cancer," says Marcel Boisvert. "War doesn't distinguish between man, woman, and child."

PERSPECTIVE: JOE CICCARELLO'S STORY

The winter of 1945 was absolutely freezing at Stalag 9B, a hilltop POW camp outside the spa town of Bad Orb. You could tell the Southern boys, says Joe Ciccarello, from the hard way they shivered, like they were going to fly apart. Joe had grown up in the North End of Boston, where February winds off the harbor bit like a shark's teeth, so he could take it better than most.

He was also prepared for starvation—if anyone can be—by a hungry childhood. Funny thing that, since his father pushed a peddler's cart heavy with fruits and vegetables up and down Hanover Street. Joe and his brothers and sisters got their fair shares of sweet corn, tomatoes, and bananas, but it just didn't stick to scrawny Joe. When he returned from school weak and woozy, his mom would crack a raw egg in a glass of sweet vermouth or muscatel, just for him, and he would swallow it down.

"A quick fix if you're out of sorts," says Joe, now 78 years old and struggling, he insists, with his memory. The dates and names might waver, we will concede that, but his recollections come forth with snap and vigor: the Franciscan nuns cracking bamboo sticks across the palms, reluctantly offered, of students caught talking in class; the special pizzas that the Regina's owners made for Joe after hours, with gobs of homemade sausage or tuna; the steeple of the Old North Church, visible from the house where he was born on Salem Street, with its high window where one lantern transmitted war intelligence to Paul Revere; and his dad's cart like a movable island of plenty. Sometimes Joe stood by the cart while the old man took a break, and he knew it was safe because "there was always someone watching out for you," in the old neighborhood.

Stuck in 9B for 80 days, Joe had time to think about everything. There was not much else to do. He became angry a lot—and that was not him, Joe was not the fuming type. Truth is, he was not angry so much at the Germans, but more at himself for the mistake that got him captured in the first

Joe Ciccarello

place. Going back for that blanket did not make sense once you looked at it from a distance, once you saw things through the wire. Once you felt your body waste to the point you could reach your hand around your thigh, all the way, and touch thumb to middle finger.

The two sergeants, you see, were not bad guys for sergeants. Joe got to know them training with the 70th Division at Fort McClellan. As they prepared to ship out of Boston in the fall of 1944, he took the sergeants to the Regina in exchange for a one-day pass. Those good ol' boys had a real pizza for the first time and, man, they loved it! Maybe it was the boat waiting, war bound, at Commonwealth Pier, or the way old friends at the Regina were looking at him in his uniform, or maybe it was just watching the sergeants savor the food as if it were their last meal, but Joe can still taste that pizza. "One of the best I ever had," he says.

During a break from training in Alabama, in June 1944, company clown Joe Ciccarello poses as a "Sad Sack" Napoleon.

The next day Joe and the sergeants—he cannot remember their names for the life of him—shipped to Marseilles, France, on the USS *United States*. It was the fastest ship afloat, marvels Joe, so fast it did not need an escort to protect it against Nazi submarines. By January their division was put on

the line in Alsace-Lorraine, where they endured the brunt of Hitler's south-
ward thrust during the Battle of the Bulge. The 70th fought back tena-
ciously, retaking the village of Wingen sur Moder and liberating a group
of just-captured Americans.

Days later in the Vosges Mountains, though, Joe's regiment was overrun
on Hill 1538 by overwhelming German forces. This was no "skirmish" in
the lingo of the history books. They engaged no "small pockets of resis-
tance"—it was a deluge of artillery, mortars, and machine-gun fire—nothing small, and definitely not pockets. Joe makes this point emphatically.
On the retreat, he came upon his sergeants in a clearing.

One of them had fallen face down, his legs shot off. You could see how a
burp gun had just sawed him off at the waist. The other sergeant lay on his
back, staring up. His stomach was open, guts spilled out, blood all over
the grass. Joe had never seen men wounded so badly; he had never seen anything so awful. And there was absolutely nothing he could do. The sergeants
might be dead already. Gunfire ripped the air.

There was nothing he could do, but "I just had to do something," says
Joe. He had noticed a blanket in the woods about fifty feet back, lying there.
So he turned around and ran to get it. He could put the blanket over the sergeant's stomach, he reasoned—he could at least do that. "I knew them," he
says. "I had broken bread with those men."

As he picked up the blanket he heard a shout in German and looked up
into the muzzle of a rifle. Behind the muzzle stood a German soldier, and
he does not have a clue why the man had not shot him. Joe surrendered
and he was marched to the rear and interrogated. ("Why do you fight for
the British?" asked a German sergeant in perfect English; the man seemed
sincerely perplexed. Did you not fight the Limeys in your Revolution?) They
shipped him by sealed boxcar to 9B.

Someone died standing up in the middle of the car and could not be lowered down. They were in there cheek to jowl, arms pinned at the sides, for
days massed tighter than rush hour commuters in the Boston subway—and
then the sound of engines started low and faraway and grew shrill as Allied
planes strafed the tracks. Pressed up against the side of the boxcar, Joe
looked through a slit in the wood and watched meadows and fields go by.
It took his mind off things, he says.

Stalag 9B was stocked with Americans, Brits, Canadians, French, Italians,
Serbians, and Senegalese, to name just a few kinds of humans. The men
from Senegal were very black, Joe remembers, and he had never even heard
of a country called Serbia. The camp menu: grass soup, black bread, and not
much else. Because there were no mirrors in the camp, Joe gauged his body's
dissolution by testing his thigh with his hand (he departed 9B almost half
gone, around sixty-five pounds, "like I'd stepped out of a ghost story"),
and he watched bombers flying east to burn Frankfurt or diving over the hill

Before shipping to France, Joe Ciccarello took two sergeants from his unit for pizza at the Regina restaurant in Boston's North End. Later he watched the two men die in battle and has been haunted by the event ever since.

to smash Bad Orb. The French bombed the camp by mistake once, impelling Joe to jump into a mud puddle.

And he thought about the blanket, the sergeants.

"I made a mistake, I shouldn't have run back," he told himself. "You're not supposed to do things like that." It went completely against his training. (When he returned home he learned the obvious, that the sergeants had died that day.) Why, he asked himself over and over, did I run back for that blanket? What was I thinking? What good could it have done?

In the camp his anger bled into guilt and shame. "All POWs felt shame," says Joe. "Just the fact that we were captured." After the war, at the lithography company where he had worked as a teenager, people called him a coward. The ones who said it had not served—isn't that the way—but it hurt like hell anyway.

The worst thing about 9B, next to starving, was the lice. They swarmed over Joe's body and hatched in the padding of his clothes. One time the Germans baked their clothes, like pizzas in an oven. Joe spent hours scratching and killing the little buggers, and he is grateful they did not leave lasting scars. That is one of Joe's humble talents, gratitude. That he never got trench foot, he is grateful for that, too. And most of all, that he kept going. Not everyone did; there was a kid in the bunk next to Joe who just stopped one day. "Didn't talk, didn't do anything, sat there in his own excrement," he remembers. They took the boy away and God knows what happened after that. Only 14 years old, the poor sap had used his older brother's ID to get into the infantry.

Camp life was tedium, broken by work details to gather firewood for the potbellied stove in the barracks. Joe received one shower in 80 days, near the end, cold and quick. He sent two pieces of mail and received exactly none back. All in all, the guards treated the POWs all right. "Wait, wait," they advised the prisoners, and perhaps themselves. "Americans on the way." Hoping, of course, it was not the damn Russians. Occasionally, a dozen POWs got to divvy up a Red Cross package; some men, sad to say, begged for more than their share.

Starvation blunted every other concern, made men hard. When it was his turn to cut the daily loaf of bread, to be evenly divided between 15 POWs, Joe remembers "those 14 faces looking at me like they wanted to kill me if I made a mistake." Once, after going all day without food, he pronounced out loud, "How long does it take to starve to death?" It was the question everyone kept inside.

Then there was that time two Americans snuck into the kitchen for food and attacked a guard with an axe. The Germans made the entire camp stand outside in the freezing cold all day, until the offenders were found out. Not one of the POWs spoke up for them and they were never heard from again, as far as Joe knows.

On April 2, 1945, American forces liberated the camp. They told the POWs to stay, but Joe beelined it into town for food. First thing he swallowed: a raw egg, cracked right down the hatch, just like old times. Then he walked up to an American tank and yelled, "Anyone here from Boston?" Up popped the tank commander and wouldn't you know it, there was Joe Greco from the North End. After the war, the two Joes made it a habit to go out for scotch and sodas every April 2, their Liberation Day. A few years ago, not long before he died, Joe Greco moved into Joe Ciccarello's apartment building and they spent a lot of time together, reminiscing.

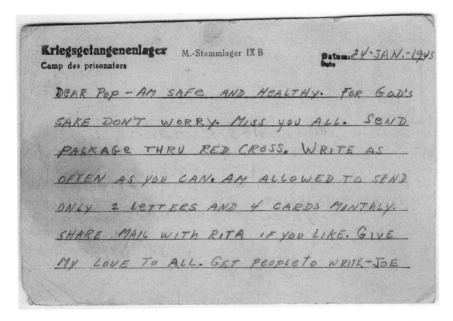

Kriegsgefangenenlager M.-Stammlager IX B   Datum: 24-JAN-1945
Camp des prisonniers

DEAR POP - AM SAFE AND HEALTHY. FOR GOD'S
SAKE DON'T WORRY. MISS YOU ALL. SEND
PACKAGE THRU RED CROSS. WRITE AS
OFTEN AS YOU CAN. AM ALLOWED TO SEND
ONLY 2 LETTERS AND 4 CARDS MONTHLY.
SHARE MAIL WITH RITA IF YOU LIKE. GIVE
MY LOVE TO ALL. GET PEOPLE TO WRITE - JOE

Joe sent this postcard to his father from Stalag IXB. In it he mentions his high school
sweetheart Rita, but their relationship fizzled after the war. "I enjoyed my freedom,"
says Joe.

In 1945, back home safe but not sound, Joe's nightmare started. It went
like this. He lies in the streets of a big city like Boston, staring up, and the
buildings converge at their tips—a trick of perspective—as if moving to a
vanishing point. Like trees do when you lie on the ground in an old forest
and look up. Then the sky fills with thousands and thousands of planes,
wings nearly touching, and the bombs fall toward Joe, hurtling down and
growing bigger and bigger in his eyes. He always wakes with a startle before
they explode. He always lives.

Fortunately, within a few years Joe's nightmare faded. It has only resur-
faced a few times. The guilt about his capture, though, stayed for a very long
time—even though feeling guilty made less sense than going back for that
blanket. He knows that, but knowing only goes so far. There is what should
be, and what is.

In time Joe got married, fathered three children, and built a sturdy life. He
decided to become a photographer, so he trained at the Eastern School of
Photography (his daughter teaches there now, he says proudly) and opened
a commercial studio on Hanover Street with an Irish buddy from Chelsea.
Nine to five, walk-ins accepted. Snappy portraits for school, confirmations,
you name it. It took a long time for Joe to get the knack, though, for helping

people relax in front of the camera, for capturing their good sides. And for relaxing, himself, behind the camera.

"There are so many mistakes you can make in photography," he asserts. He does not mention all the things you can do right. Sometimes it's what you do wrong that sticks the hardest.

On the side, Joe took photos of the cooks and waiters and customers at the Regina. It was the least he could do—"They were so good to me," he says—and the photos went up on the walls, food for hungry eyes. He does not know the folks who own the Regina these days, after all this time, but he still likes to take his friends there. A couple of his old photos are still hanging. In the back corner there is a fine shot, one of his best, of men hoisting beers at a nearby bar.

The studio lasted for 20 years until a new job came along. And so for the next 20 years Joe soared aloft in helicopters, photographing landscapes for the state Department of Public Works. On his photos they drew silver ribbons where the new roads would go. It made him feel useful, helping to make things new.

Now Joe puts out a couple of glasses, each with a raw egg floating in sweet vermouth. He and a visitor gulp them down. "That's good, isn't it?" he says.

THE TWO EISENHOWERS: JOE CANAVAN'S STORY

Months after D-Day and not long before his capture during the Battle of the Bulge, Joe Canavan and the other wandering souls in his "bastard battalion" of combat engineers were sent to Brittany to repair an airfield. They were used to shuttling among divisions—building corduroy roads through muck and mud, laying down Bailey bridges—anything to smooth the battlefield, keep the war moving. On this day a cargo plane landed, probably a C-47, says Joe, and "out popped Eisenhower."

General Dwight D. Eisenhower, Supreme Commander of Allied Forces, plain as day. He brought his personal jeep on the plane, remembers Joe, and he wore his trademark khaki coat, cut short above his trim waist. Ike said hello to the troops in a quiet voice and shook a few hands. Joe was lucky to have his camera and snapped the general smiling and waving, just a few yards away. He could have touched the old man. But when the photos came back from the Army developing lab, the Eisenhower shots were gone. Maybe they were removed for the usual paranoid security reasons. Maybe someone swiped them for a souvenir.

"I'd sure like to get my hands on those photos," says Joe.

It is now 60 years later. Joe sounds frustrated, as if the foul-up happened yesterday. But resigned, too. The photos are long gone and some things you just have to accept—like what happened to the boys who stormed Utah Beach instead of Joe. He was supposed to go on D-Day, supposed to move in

Joe Canavan

ahead of the infantry and clear antipersonnel mines, but a soldier in his unit contracted meningitis and they scratched everyone. Their replacements, the 59th Combat Engineer Division, lost 95 percent of their men on Utah Beach. Joe did not know anything about that, though, when he and his fellow bastards went ashore a few weeks later.

Sometimes not knowing is best, says Joe. For instance, take his capture on December 21, 1944, following five days of unholy onslaught by Nazi troops that left his unit encircled behind the lines. He did not have a clue what he was in for next. "I'm glad I didn't know," he states emphatically.

"I was just relieved to get out of it, to tell you the truth. I felt exhilarated. No more guns, no more shooting." In the back of his mind, he pictured the German POWs who had done his laundry at Camp Carson in Colorado. They looked well treated and were even allowed to play soccer. The rumors about concentration camps and mistreatment of Allied prisoners had not gotten back to Joe.

First he was shipped to Stalag 12A outside Limburg. There he and other men from his company washed off in a large shower room—it felt good at the time. A Christmas present. The horror hit him later, in retrospect, when he learned about the Holocaust. Joe saw a photo of the shower rooms where Jews were lured and gassed, and he recognized the shower heads in those rooms, the exact same kind of shower heads that had sprayed water, not poisonous gas, on him. Water, because he was an American. He still wonders what he would have done in the Jews' place. He thinks about how he would have reacted, in the shower rooms without water.

Next they were marched to a camp in Gerolstein, a little factory town where "I worked my ass off," states Joe, filling in bomb craters and carrying water. The POWs watched American P-47s fly over on bombing runs. Each man got a slice of bread in the morning, a ladle of miserable soup at night. In Gerolstein, Joe Canavan witnessed a second Eisenhower in action.

This Eisenhower may have spelled his name Eisenhauer—the same spelling used by General Eisenhower's German ancestors in the eighteenth century. It means "iron worker" or, more literally, "one who beats on metal." This Eisenhower, a sergeant in the guard, was a tall man with a pointy face and stern expression. He dressed like an officer, his cap shiny, a leather crop gripped in his hand. He was in his late twenties, probably. "An old man to us," says Joe.

One day Sergeant Eisenhower had trouble rousing prisoners for a work detail, which was strange, Joe adds, because they were starving and details were good for scrounging food. The guard became furious. He took out a Luger and approached an American POW laying flat in his bunk. He put the gun to the boy's head and shot him dead. Then he walked away and they never saw him again.

After the war, Joe reported the atrocity to Army intelligence. He heard a rumor that they got him, the second Eisenhower, but he does not really know. He would like to know; it was a long time ago, though, and many days have passed.

Things only got worse. Joe was packed in a train and moved to Stalag 9B at Bad Orb, considered one of the worst POW camps in Germany. His barracks had no bunks. For two months the men slept on the floor, in mud and filth. It was the middle of the winter. They had no blankets and huddled together in fetal positions. Warm up one side, turn over, warm up the other. Red Cross packages did not arrive. Often the prisoners were locked in the barracks all day. The dysentery Joe had picked up on his first day of capture, from drinking water out of his soap-encrusted helmet, attacked him without mercy. His malnutrition reached a severe stage, and in desperation he traded his class ring and his gold Bulova watch to a Russian for a slice of bread with jelly. His skin sagged off his bones.

"We were too weak to work," says Joe. "The living dead." Every week he thought he would not last one more week. The body ruled the mind. "You're in limbo and food is all you can think about. We sat together and

Joe Canavan as a young soldier.

drew up menus...turkey dinners with all the fixings...we dreamed of meals."

Joe Canavan, however, was not some pampered kid raised on a bursting fridge. He grew up in an Irish Catholic household in South Boston, one of eight children. The Canavans struggled during the Depression, eating haddock bought off horse and wagons or caught by Joe at the Castle Island pier. "We never lived high on the hog," he says. The Army, actually, was a godsend. He entered at 127 pounds and ate so well and so often that he beefed up to 150. In captivity Joe believes that he lived off that extra body fat. On the day after Easter, 1945, when a Russian tank broke down the gate at Bad Orb and the tank commander tossed cigarettes from his perch like candy off a parade float, he stood there a 93-pound skeleton.

A happy skeleton, on the day after Easter. "It was a resurrection, all right," says Joe, laughing.

He and a fellow POW named Norman Rogers located some horsemeat. Joe nibbled a little bit, but Norman gobbled down a big portion. "I don't care if it kills me," he said, and the next morning he was moaning terribly. They took him to a hospital and Joe could not help thinking, "He's gonzo." Later he heard a rumor about a POW who wolfed down a half dozen donuts and dropped dead on the spot. But a few years after the war, out of the blue, Norman showed up at Joe's door just to say hello.

Then they were brought to an airfield and deloused. The men stripped off their mangy clothes, which were taken away for burning, and Joe remembers seeing, as if for the first time, the lice that had infested his body from the neck down. His fingertips were stained bloody brown from picking at them. No lice in his hair, though—strange, because as a kid the lice *only* got in his hair. Hard to figure, like so many other things.

At Camp Lucky Strike, the rehab camp in France for released POWs, Joe took in soup and gruel for weeks. Slowly he felt himself getting stronger. In May he boarded a troop ship in Le Havre, bound for home, and right away he volunteered for typing duty in the captain's mess. "Never volunteer for nothing, you learn that first day in the Army," says Joe, but not this time. This duty got him special meal passes. His job was to type a list of every POW and wounded man aboard, name after name for the Western Union telegraph man, and he did it nice and easy, all the time eating whatever and whenever he liked, no questions asked. Two weeks later the ship sailed into New York Harbor.

His voice shimmers in the telling: "I can see it in my mind right now. Dawn's breaking, and there's the outline of the Statue of Liberty. You could hear a pin drop. The most beautiful sight I ever saw."

And that was that. No band waited on the dock, no newsreel cameras recorded their safe return. Of his homecoming, Joe remembers most of all being told by Army officials not to talk about his POW experience. Get on with your life; people will not understand. Then he learned about the shower heads that poured gas, not water, and he learned about how the 95th Combat Engineers were slaughtered in his place on Utah Beach. He read about the triumphant Eisenhower and wondered, What happened to those photos? Did they still exist somewhere? And he thought about the second Eisenhower with the leather crop and the Luger, the way he had moved so swiftly to murder the sleeping soldier, then turned and left the barracks.

Joe moved in with his parents and it was no surprise that he started drinking, heavily. He bummed around for years, not much good to anyone until he met his wife Marilyn at a party on White Horse Beach in 1952.

"She turned me around," says Joe. For the next 30 years he worked as a bridge inspector and part time at a supermarket, and he put two children

U. S. Department of Justice

Foreign Claims Settlement Commission
of the United States

Washington, D.C. 20579

May 27, 1998

Mr. Joseph T. Canavan
24 Middlesex Circle, Apt. 9
Waltham, MA 02154-6240

                                Re: Claim No. HS-165

Dear Mr. Canavan:

        In the course of completing its work on the Holocaust
Survivors Claims Program, the Foreign Claims Settlement Commission
has again carefully reviewed your letter concerning the
Commission's August 14, 1997 decision on your claim.

        We recognize that the conditions you and your comrades endured
in the POW camps must have been deplorable. Indeed, Stalag 9B at
Bad Orb was reputedly the worst of the Nazi POW camps.

        Unfortunately, as the Commission's *Final Decision on the Scope
of the Holocaust Survivors Claims Program* discussed, Germany has
agreed -- with very minor exceptions, not applicable in your case
-- to cover only the claims of those who were interned in
"concentration camps" or "sub-camps" *recognized as such by Germany*.
At page 13, the Final Decision on Scope also explained that "the
Commission has no power to declare institutions *de facto*
concentration camps." Regrettably, POW camps are not recognized as
concentration camps or sub-camps by Germany; and the Commission
remains bound by the limits of Germany's agreement.

        The Commission recognizes that Germany's terms mean that many
Holocaust survivors who endured horrific conditions will not be
compensated in this claims program. Unfortunately, however, the
Commission can take no further action on your claim.

        To you and the other ex-POWs who sacrificed so much in the
service of your country, we owe a tremendous debt of gratitude. We
deeply regret that we cannot respond more favorably to your letter.

                        Sincerely,

                        Sebastian Saviano
                        Special Assistant
                          to the Chair

Joe Canavan's claim against Germany for the abuse he endured at Stalag 9B was rejected in this letter from the U.S. Department of Justice.

through college. One of his grandchildren has recently joined ROTC at Boston College and he believes it will be good for her: "You can't tell a teenager anything. I told the wife, she'll get a little discipline." He says it gruffly, with a kind of false conviction, because, after all, you cannot know how these things will turn out. The wife, he adds, worries that the girl will be sent to Iraq or Afghanistan or some godforsaken place and never come back.

And even if you return, if you survive the hell, it can almost be like you had not. Christmas and Easter, the poles of capture and liberation, bring especially dark and depressing thoughts for Joe Canavan. It is not as if he has not tried to set things right, fill in the missing spaces. In 1997, through the U.S. Justice Department, he filed Claim No. HS-165 against "the government of the Federal Republic of Germany." The Foreign Claims Settlement Commission was not unsympathetic, acknowledging in a letter that Joe had been "subject to persistent hunger, hard labor, and constant brutal treatment" and "to this day he continues to suffer from extreme anxiety, flashbacks, and sleep disorders." Unfortunately, "this claim is not compensable here... the places he was held are not recognized by ITS or BGBI as concentration camps or sub-camps." Signed, Richard T. White, Commissioner.

Counseling has helped, certainly, and he always enjoys meeting with other ex-POWs (though he gets out less since his hip acted up). Joe confides that he even took an antidepressant for awhile—on top of the pills for blood pressure, high cholesterol, you name it. The strange thing is, despite everything, he is outliving his brothers and sisters. Several years ago he lost five of his six sisters in the same year. One after the other, five of them, dead and gone. That was not easy to bear.

Fifteen years ago Joe returned to Europe with a group of World War II veterans and former POWs. To get it out of his system, he told himself.

They visited Portsmouth, England, a staging point for D-Day. Joe had been ready to go, primed, but a man cannot fight off meningitis, you cannot shoot a bug like that with a gun. You have to wait. Then Joe and a few others from his bastard battalion read a plaque on Utah Beach, commemorating the men of the 59th Combat Engineer Division, wiped out in their stead, and they revisited sites all along their wandering wartime route: St. Lo, bombed to a shell; Paris, where they gave candy bars to little French kids on the condition they belt out *La Marseillaise;* the submarine pens in Brest, where he and buddies threw explosives called potato mashers off the docks (you had to have some fun); and the airfield in Brittany where he took those photos, those long-lost photos of the good Eisenhower as he smiled and waved—and then over the Rhine at Remagen and right up to the foxhole imprints, now smooth and grassy and almost imperceptible, in the ground where he was captured.

There he stopped. No further on the war trail; it had been too much misery beyond that point. Still, he knows this much. "We lucked out," says Joe.

CHAPTER 2

Acceptance and Adaptation

PERPETUAL MOTION: COSMO FABRIZIO'S STORY

It is no good anymore walking on hard surfaces—the pain sears his arches in memory of long slogs through the winter of 1945, burlap bags for socks and shoes—but that does not mean he has stopped moving.

At age 82, Cosmo Fabrizio still cuts his grass, as well as his neighbor's (the poor guy has one lung). He walks two miles every morning, six o'clock a.m., in the forgiving sand of a beach not far from his home at Plymouth Mobile Estates. A mile down and a mile back. "That salt air, delicious," he says. He likes to take his iron rake and go clamming—even in the winter—down at the coastal flats in Duxbury, and he steams the clams himself and serves them up with olive oil and garlic on beds of spaghetti. Cosmo has intense, restless eyes, and while he looks comfortable enough sitting down, surrounded by keepsakes and his wife Louise's homey decorating touches, there is also the sense that he might bound out of his chair at any moment.

In fact, he does a few times. Once to slash the room in half with his arms —that's all the space they had in the boxcar they rode from Stalag XIIA, a transit camp, to Stalag IIIC east of Berlin. More than 100 men, all privates, were "crammed like sardines, you couldn't fall down if you wanted to," says Cosmo. It took 23 days to make the 185-mile trip from Limburg to Kustrine, the train constantly backing up to avoid track destroyed by Allied bombing. Each man had about five day's meager rations, "Kraut rations" they called them. Men died standing up. In a fenced-off area of the boxcar, the German guards enjoyed the unimaginable luxury of sitting in chairs and eating hot food.

Cosmo Fabrizio

"It was horrendous, guys dropping right next to you. You figured you were next." He survived, says Cosmo, with "prayers, hope, memories." He thought about childhood spaghetti dinners with his family in the Bronx. About high school graduation and playing basketball and baseball. He was lucky to make a friend on the train, Dick Conright, and they slept against each other standing up. Cosmo said the Lord's Prayer.

He rises again, this time to fetch his snappy Eisenhower jacket. It is part of the uniform he was issued after his liberation, after his surreal, wrong-way trek back to Allied lines. The jacket still fits, he insists, and he shows off not the medals, not the rows of insignia, but his Honorable Service lapel pin over the breast pocket. It is an eagle, wings outstretched, inside a wreath. Cosmo calls it a "ruptured duck." Why a duck? He does not know; everyone called it that. It meant you were discharged and home free. Gone like a ruptured duck!

"I didn't like the Army, but I did my job and that's it," he says. "When I got that ruptured duck, boy, I felt better than the president."

He earned that duck. Cosmo was 19 years old and trucking waste paper around New York when he was drafted in the spring of 1942. Courtesy of

Cosmo Fabrizio calls his much-prized discharge badge a
"ruptured duck." He took the phrase from soldier lingo:
"I'm out of here like a ruptured duck."

Uncle Sam, he took a two-year tour of the USA, pulling duty at bases in
North Carolina, Georgia, Louisiana, Oregon, and California. It was
D-Day by the time his division finally shipped out and he did not get to
spend more than two days in England at a "repo depot"—a gathering point
for replacement soldiers, as if they were spare parts—before landing in
France.

Cosmo's unit fired 60mm mortars from relative safety behind the lines. St.
Lo fell, providing a break in the German defenses around Normandy, and
they marched like crazy with Patton's army toward Paris. ("It was our blood
and his guts," says Cosmo about Patton. "But he was a brilliant leader.")
Events, though, took a dicey turn at the aptly named Purple Heart Hill.
Cosmo the mortar man became an instant sergeant-on-the-line, leading a
squad of eight. Here his greatest fear, touched off the moment he landed in
France, grew more threatening: that he would be killed by *Allied* bombing,
specifically from "close support" sorties that could miss the mark and result
in what Bomber Command called "short bombing" or "totally misplaced
concentrations." Cosmo did not like the idea of dying by royal screw-up,
of getting dismembered because some general wanted to try a new battlefield strategy.

Allied bombing failed to get them, but German fire did kill three men in
the squad. A piece of shrapnel sliced to the bone of Cosmo's right foot. Surrounded in a bomb crater, he saw no good choice but to surrender himself
and the surviving men under his command. He did not expect to ever see
home again.

So Cosmo Fabrizio was packed away into the backwaters of the war, into
the holding pens of the Thousand Year Reich. Thousands of Americans

shared Stalag IIIC with Russian, British, and Italian prisoners. The Russians were treated the worse, Cosmo remembers, worked like slaves until they dropped dead.

Cosmo and 60 American POWs slept on racks in a cramped hut. The latrine, a bucket at one end, stunk up the place. As the winter of 1944 descended, they ripped wood from the ceiling to stoke their Sibley potbelly stove. The Germans treated Cosmo's shrapnel wound with sulfur and wrapped it with crepe paper as a bandage. But the right boot was gone and he had to wrap burlap around the foot to protect it.

The radio made a big difference. An ingenious kid rigged it from a sewing needle, a double-edged razor, and wire plugged into a light socket. At night, after roll call and grass soup and sawdust bread, they listened to the faint signal of the BBC in shifts, the men huddled over the delicate gizmo. "It kept us going," says Cosmo. Their spirits sagged, though, when they learned about the Allies getting creamed in the Battle of the Bulge. So much for the rumor about the war ending by Christmas.

"That's it," Cosmo remembers thinking. "Goodbye, Charlie."

Those damn roll calls, they never ended. Morning, noon, and night. Stand and wait, stand and wait. The POWs grew weak, light as birds—Cosmo's weight dropped from 140 to 95 pounds during his captivity. All that time he saw one lousy Red Cross package, ripped open by six men. Time dripped, life was dull. Sometimes they were allowed to toss a baseball around or walk the camp grounds. Stripped to the waist, the men picked lice off each other's bodies, and they made elaborate, tunneling escape plans that went nowhere. The floors of the huts were raised above the ground, allowing the guards to keep an eye on that kind of business.

The German sergeant in charge of their hut spoke pretty good English. Believe it or not, he said he was from Brooklyn, said he rooted for the Dodgers. The way he told it, he came to Germany to visit relatives in the late 1930s and the army nabbed him. The man had a slight German accent that muffled the Brooklyn in his voice—who knows, maybe he told the truth, says Cosmo. Or maybe he was programmed by his superiors to deceive the prisoners. Either way, Russian troops who liberated the camp on February 5, 1945, shoved Sergeant Brooklyn and all the guards into the camp bakery and machine-gunned them down.

Those Russkie soldiers, says Cosmo, were drunk as hell. They roared into camp in tanks and a woman got out of the lead one—what a tough broad! Some of the prisoners offered to join forces against the Germans, but the Russians turned them down. The POWs were forced to give blood—the nurse knew two words of English: "Hold still!"—and then were let loose, abandoned to find their own ways home.

West did not work, into the fighting. North or south, just as bad. So, by default, approximately 2,000 Americans broke into small groups and headed east across Germany. Cosmo and his pal Dick Conright scrounged

Cosmo Fabrizio as a young soldier.

food from deserted farmhouses. They rode bikes until they broke, stole cars and drove them dry. Once they hopped a train but got off when they realized it was rolling toward Moscow. Inside one barn, Cosmo saw a family lined up neatly on the ground, children to parents to grandparents, each with a bullet hole between the eyes.

"The Russians were as bad as the Germans," he says.

Somehow he and Dick got split up and, for the first time in his life, Cosmo found himself alone. You didn't get much privacy in a big family, or in the Army, and certainly not in the death trains or POW camps. But now, with the Russian war machine streaming past on all sides, Cosmo was alone.

The boot on his left foot shredded apart. The shrapnel wound in his right foot was killing him. With *both* feet wrapped in burlap now, he wandered down the frozen roads of Poland. In Posnan, fortunately, he met a family that washed his clothes and served him his first good meal in ages. A friendly Russian truck driver offered him a glass of vodka which he thought was water, and it made him sick for three days. Villagers gave him food as soon as they saw the American flag on his field jacket. "Essen, essen," he would say, pointing at his open mouth. "Amerikanski, essen!"

One day Cosmo walked up the crest of a hill and saw Warsaw burning. He took a good look at the ruins, at the smoking devastation that the retreating Germans had wrought as Russian troops, on Stalin's orders, stood back and let happen, and he decided to take a wide berth around the city.

Relentlessly walking and hitching rides, Cosmo traveled southeast through Central Europe and arrived, finally, at the port of Odessa on the Black Sea—a thousand-mile trek from Stalag IIIC. That same day he was corralled by Russian police—all women, more tough broads!—and stowed in a hollowed-out school with other GIs straggling into the city. But there was no stopping him now. Cosmo climbed aboard a British "liberty boat" and cruised across the Black Sea, through the Dardanelles, and into the blue Aegean and Mediterranean Seas. The ship lit in Naples, Italy, where he tried the spaghetti—not bad, but he liked his mother's better, served up with heapings of relatives in the Bronx.

After debriefing and medical treatment, Cosmo was given a choice. You can go home, they offered, or join an outfit fighting in Germany. Not on your life, or mine, he told them. "I came through it all in pretty good shape. Why tempt fate a second time?" When he finally arrived home, in Boston, he kneeled and kissed the ground.

The moment he stood up, just about, Cosmo started dating Louise, a girl he had known before the war, and by September 1945 he got his ruptured duck. (He would have been sent to the Pacific War, if not for the atomic bombs dropped in August.) Finally, he was sprung, no need to wait around anymore, and he put his mind to job one: convince Louise to marry him, and soon. He wanted to tie the knot before the New Year, but she said, Gus, let's wait and see (she calls him Gus, like his grandmother did in her broken English). "She was yes and no, yes and no," says Cosmo. "I told her, 'What's holding you up?'" Nothing, in the end, and they were married with two days to spare in 1945. Next thing you know Louise was pregnant with a boy, Michael, now a medical doctor.

Cosmo made up for lost time, and fast.

Never one to settle down at a desk, of course, he worked mostly in mobile catering, driving a canteen truck until retirement. Forty-three stops a day, he says, proudly. That's 43 starts, too. Forty-three new chances. Cosmo knew to keep moving—after all, there is freedom in movement, sweet freedom. So every single day he is on the beach, six o'clock in the morning, walking in the forgiving sand. A mile down and a mile back. At the same time, Louise strolls in a nearby park.

It is not that he seeks to deny the darkness of his ordeal. But he does not want that darkness to overshadow him, either. So Cosmo keeps moving, the best he can. "You never forget about it, but you try to," he says.

Cosmo Fabrizio

IN THE BARON'S BOWLING ALLEY: JOHN LUPONE'S STORY

"It's so easy for one little thing to change your life completely, isn't it?" says John Lupone, a man with a fine-honed sense of fate's trickery during wartime, when a soldier's life is cheap and beyond his control. His World War II tale pivots on this insight, exposing the strange and ironic power of minor events in the realm of chaos.

John Lupone

Given this way of seeing—common among POWs bent on figuring it out —some men chew for decades on gristly "what if's" and "why me's," growing glum with wondering, but that's not for John. His war, the whole damn thing, still amazes him, still makes him shake his head with a smile, from the supply bags stuck in the plane door on D-Night to the P-38s that could not smash that stubborn bridge to the vengeful, buggering British sergeant major who saved his skin at Stalag 4B. He laughs a lot in the telling because, well, it is pretty funny if you allow it to be.

First off, take the storm that flooded the Potomac River in the fall of 1942. John sits on a troop train going from Boston to Miami. Halfway there the Potomac overflows and they are diverted to Fort Bragg, North Carolina. Instead of duty in the Army Air Corps, John is tabbed for a battlefield medic and just like that, haphazard, he is sticking needles in oranges, learning the parts of the body. It's all make-believe, though. His first opportunity to treat a real person will have to come in combat. Later in '43, the 101st Airborne Division arrives on base and John, what do you know, finds himself as a parachuting medic.

OK by him. He is glad to avoid serving with the glider boys (plywood caskets, he calls the gliders) and gets to strut with the elite Airborne. "We lorded it over the regular army," he recalls, chuckling. "We were top choice."

Not that he doesn't take his lumps. John receives a three-day pass in July and hightails it home to Somerville, Massachusetts, to visit family and friends. It might be his last chance before shipping out, maybe his last chance ever. Admits John, "I went over the hill." Three days extends to seven and when he gets back to Fort Bragg he is given three months' "company duty" cleaning barracks and shoveling coal, with no pay. The sentence overlaps with his unit's transfer overseas to a base outside of London in August 1944.

"It was easy punishment," laughs John. "We had our own room, and the lock was on the inside of the door. Sometimes we'd send the guard to the kitchen to get us food late at night."

In the fall, he loves jump school: "It's a beautiful sight when you're out of the plane, nice and quiet, floating down with the chute only." Night jumping, he realizes, is like falling into a dark well. Up high you can see the outlines of things, the landscape of sky and earth, but the closer you get to the ground the blacker it becomes. The blackness tells you to bend your knees, if you do not want your legs broken. Another trick: make a quarter turn toward the tail when you step out of the plane, so your lines do not slash your face. John forgets this on a practice jump and loses the feeling in one ear for a month.

And England is a lark! He goes with a girl working on a farm in the Women's Land Army, nothing serious, and he shines the tight beam of his blackout flashlight up the gams of gals on the street. On leave in London, John stands in a doorway during a bombing raid, listening to the "tinkle, tinkle, tinkle of the roof slates coming down…you could get your head cut off!" It is a great adventure.

June 5, 1944, 'twas the night before D-Day. John and hundreds of Airborne troops form a great circle around General Eisenhower on a landing strip in southern England. The old West Pointer gives a rah-rah speech, like they are a football team. Anxious as all hell, John nonetheless manages to sleep in the plane over the English Channel, a bundle of morphine and bandages and pep pills strapped to his chest above the reserve chute. He wears an armband and a helmet with a red cross on it, and he is unarmed like all medics. Then the sergeant bellows: "On your feet, Screaming Eagles!" John looks outside at a storm of flak and it is like "the Fourth of July fireworks on the Charles River, but more of it."

Here he stops the story, at the most exciting part, to deliver a monologue on the ingenious double zippers running horizontally across his jump suit, designed so either hand could pull out a knife for cutting the chute lines once you make ground. John is sitting on a couch with flowered cushions in a sunny, enclosed porch overlooking his backyard. There is a tall weeping willow out there; sometimes coyotes mill about under the branches. What

At home on a three-day pass he stretched to a week in 1943, John (front right) horses around with his best buddies (left to right in rear): friend Robert Luti, cousin Eddie Lupone, and brother Americo.

a beautiful spot, except for the thrum of traffic on Route 93 beyond the trees. The area was farmland when he bought the house 50 years ago and nobody mentioned a highway. File that under you-never-know-what-you're-gonna-get.

So it's jump-time, and they kick the supply bags out first. But the damn things stick in the doorframe and they have a devil of a time getting them free. That is why he misses his drop zone and comes down in a field dag-gered with stakes for smashing gliders. That is why his lines get tangled on a stake, why his chute billows up and down like a surrender flag, and why a German soldier on bicycle patrol sticks a gun in his face before he can pull in his gear. Why he never used his medic's training, not once. If not for the supply bags, a different future might have met John Lupone—he might be dead, for that matter.

Over several days John and hundreds of Allied POWs—including Brits, Canadians, South Africans, New Zealanders—are marched down the Cher-bourg Peninsula to a monastery they called Starvation Hill. The monks have bugged out. Two crazy things happen there. First, John finds a swarm of snails stuck to a moist wall in the monks' garden. Oh, the things his mama could do with snails, simmered in a garlicky tomato sauce! He collects them and rushes back to his starving comrades. But the U.K. boys refuse to eat up. "Trouble was," says John, laughing, "they weren't Italians."

The second crazy thing: day after day, American P-38s strafe and bomb a bridge over the river below the monastery, but somehow it will not go down. Will not budge for nothing. Turns out, that is the bridge the POWs cross in trucks, east toward Germany, and John believes they might not have been moved, might even have been liberated, if not for that ridiculous bridge. (Things look up a few days later, though, when they find a tobacco stash and smoke until their heads swim.)

Paris, you could not have seen that coming. Their train arrives at the wrong station, so the POWs are marched through the city to another station. Along the way, French civilians kick them, punch them, and yell hatefully. John is stunned; what the heck, they are doing this to *us*? Maybe they think we jumped into this mess for our health? He remembers people peering down from windows and a radio reporter yakking into a micro-phone, transmitting news of the filthy, captured Allied soldiers back to the Fatherland.

The men are stuffed in railcars and moved to Stalag 12A, a miserable "grin and bear it" kind of place, where they remain for about six weeks. John has a couple of stories from here, each about food. You've heard of Limburger cheese? 12A is near Limburg and the POWs are given this cheese—oh my, the smell! John cannot bring himself to touch it. Hungry or not, he laughs, no way! The other tale, well, judge for yourself. Two Rus-sian prisoners escape, but are tracked down by dogs and killed. Their bodies are paraded down the main drag of the camp in wheelbarrows, for all to see. And that night, in the POWs' soup, there is more meat than ever before.

John Lupone was born in 1921 in Tocco da Casauna (Village on a Cliff) in Italy. His father, actually, lived in the United States as a citizen before World War I, but then he was drafted into the Italian army and returned to fulfill his service. Wounded fighting the Austrians, he spun right around

and settled in Boston in 1923; five years later he brought over his wife Conchita and their two children, Giovanni (John) and Philomena. Eustachio
Lupone found success working on the Boston subway, "building a name
for himself," says John, with only a second-grade education. During the
Depression, his father spread the work around to provide every man on his
crew with at least a small wage. John remembers him bringing home a
$101 check from a job, a regular king's ransom in those days.

When he turned 18 years old, John received a draft notice from the Italian
army, too. You have gotta be kidding! No going back for him!

In September 1944, John is shuffled to Stalag 4B, a camp with 30,000
prisoners in southeastern Germany. Captivity there is dull, food scarce,
and his weight plummets. The POWs listen to war news on a hidden radio
and banter through the fence with Polish female prisoners. John's glad to
get transferred out around Christmas—and it's a funny story how that
happened.

The POW commander in his barracks is a British sergeant major, an
upright dandy fellow. One day he approaches John and his American buddies at a card game and starts handing out free cigarettes. But everyone
knows his game; he is trolling for a bedmate. The Americans tell him to
shove it, scram Limey, and you would have thought he had never been

On leave at home in Massachusetts, John Lupone visited his mother,
Conchita, and his father, Eustacio, before he left for war in 1943.

John Lupone

yapped at before. Of course, that is not the end of it. The sergeant major uses his influence with the Germans to have the Americans transferred to a satellite labor camp.

That guy thought he was punishing us, crows John. That guy saved our skin! The wise-ass Americans are sent to a baron's estate where they cut logs in the forest and bunk in a spacious bowling alley behind the castle guest house. Hard to believe, a bowling alley! They are fed okay, too, enough to make it through the winter. Out in the woods, when the guards are not looking, John and his buddies pass firewood to local women, who sneak them potatoes in return.

They consider escaping, but what is the point? Where would they go? Besides, the Russians are getting closer, the guards insist. When this war ends, one of them proclaims, we are going to help you fight the Russians. John has a hard time believing that could ever happen. In February, the POWs hear an incredible pounding as nearby Dresden is destroyed from on high. "Those poor people got burned alive," laments John. He pauses for a moment. Then he changes gears, expounding upon the forest master's amazing gas-powered saw, the first one he ever saw. It was a thing of beauty.

On Friday, April 13, 1945, John and his mates are liberated by American troops. So that is a good luck day for him, Friday the 13th. And how is this for a role reversal: John guards German soldiers as they are trucked to processing centers. (It was easy duty; the Germans were delighted to be captured by Americans.) En route he gets a good look at the first combat jet, the Folke Wolf Me-262, an amazing piece of machinery. A good thing the Germans only got it in limited production, he is quick to add.

Back home, after a period of recuperation, John tries but cannot break into a mechanical field. Married now, with a kid on the way, he joins the Postal Service and stays there until 1981. Time then to enjoy retirement? Not for John—he finds work in a machine shop that churns out parts for the Patriot missile system used in the Persian Gulf War. Finally, he gets to use his high school algebra and trigonometry! Ten years later he retires and unretires again with a new job cutting grass and burying people at a Jewish cemetery. He likes the peace, the quiet, nobody bothering you much.

"It's so easy for one little thing to change your life completely, isn't it?" says John Lupone. His voice is soft and warm and somehow manages to overwhelm the unceasing din of the highway beyond the trees.

COUNT YOUR BLESSINGS: ROGER HUGHES'S STORY

"The toughest part was keeping it to yourself," says Roger Hughes, airman of the B-17 Flying Fortress, prisoner of the Third Reich (January 1944–April 1945), and son of an upright Irishman in a starched collar as white as a spring gull over Boston Harbor, as high as his unreachable aspirations. You kept it to yourself, Roger explains about the fear, the sadness, and the ache of physical wasting, you rolled it up inside because you wanted to be a regular Joe, a them's-the-breaks kind of guy.

His Tibetan terrier, Ryan, dozes on a cushion by his leg in this shingled house just east of the Cape Cod Canal. In dog years, she is a tad younger than her 84-year-old master. He talks to her, he says with a laugh, but

Roger Hughes

doesn't get a lot of answers back. Enormous holly bushes surround the front steps, a male and a female; Roger waters them every day and encourages neighbors to take snippings. Just inside the house your eyes fix upon a photograph of his deceased wife, Mary Ester Hughes, angled on a side table. It is '45 forever within the frame and her satin wedding dress trails shimmering to the horizon.

Roger sports the tight-checked flannel shirt favored by old men in New England. His running shoes are offset by black socks. But on the other hand, he declares, it was not so easy keeping it inside. And then after several digressions about his four brothers and how one became a Jesuit priest and another was 4F with a bad stomach and two took up drafting like the old man and now they are all dead but him—after looping around the block in his own sweet time, Roger Hughes declares that it made no sense to play the tough guy, either.

"Let's face it, we knew we were prisoners," says Roger. "There was no way we could lick the system."

So in Stalag 17 he learned to adjust and adapt. It was not easy, no sir, getting along in such close quarters, taking your share without grabbing for it. Ignoring the glares and sharp comments of depressed and angry POWs. Thank goodness for the letters Mary wrote and wrote and wrote—about 50 made it through. Roger let the men who did not get mail read them. This happened, that happened, miss you so, honey. The men without mail touched the paper she had touched, and they breathed in her love as if it was meant for them. He told her what he was doing, lending her out, and Mary said that she did not mind.

One letter included a black-and-white photo of Mary sitting on the granite windowsill of a building in Boston. She wears a conservative dress and her expression is a bit stiff, but her legs are crossed and dangling a la Rita Hayworth. A German censor stamped the back of the snapshot with a row of black numbers, which proves, says Roger, that he received it in the camp. The guys without mail really liked the photo, too.

Things were tight, all right: ten bays per barracks, six triple-deckered bunks per bay, two krieges per bunk. That is krieges as in *kriegsgefange,* German for POW. Some prisoners referred to themselves as krieges, as if the title of sergeant in the U.S. Air Corps had been erased and it was kriege and nothing more in this stinking hole. Other POWs said it with a bitter laugh, kriege, as in that is what they think, the stupid krauts. We will win this goddamn war. And there were those who barely spoke—like Roger's bunkmate, Warren Davis, a country kid who must have read and reread every book in the camp's meager library—but you had to respect that. It was a good idea not to judge, lest you be judged.

"I learned how to live with the masses," says Roger. He hesitates to say it, because some of his old kriege buddies might not understand, but the crammed, suffocating conditions of Stalag 17 provided him with many lessons for life. In a lot of ways, captivity was an invaluable experience.

His mother was a gentle woman, devoted to her children. And what a cook! Roger ate and ate and ate. His father, now he was plenty strict—"Daddy-O ran a tight ship," remembers Roger—and more stubborn than your average stubborn Irishman. He wanted to be called "Mr. Hughes." The wise guys at the Knights of Columbus referred to him as "The Bishop." Dad and mum were night and day, all right, black and tan. Her feet on the ground, his eyes on the sky.

"My father was meant to be better than he finally became," explains Roger. "He had the potential to be a millionaire." A while later, curling back from the story of his daughter who owned a beautiful terrier, judged best-in-show, his daughter who died last year of severe asthma—"The medicine, I swear it killed her"—at that point Roger refines the record: "If he *had* made a million dollars, that would have been the end of him."

The family lived across the harbor from Boston, in the house of his mother's father, Timothy Sullivan, who hailed from County Cork, Ireland, and did not believe in electricity. The house was lit with kerosene lamps until he fell to his death on the dark cellar stairs in 1930. Roger's father, not a backward-looking man, soon had electricity blazing in the home. For a brief period Mr. Hughes owned a factory that made windows, doors, and sashes, and he did well enough to buy a car, a rare possession on their street during the Depression.

It did not last. The union put his father out of business, according to Roger. The details are sketchy, contradictory, and it is not as if Mr. Hughes was willing to compromise in negotiations. Bottom line, it went under, and so he became a windows salesman and obsessive basement inventor. After all, if you work hard enough, anything is possible in the land of opportunity. And so was born the amazing Hughes Road Rail System.

A kind of fifth wheel and dolly contraption, the Hughes Road Rail System allowed trailers pulled by trucks to be moved directly onto rails for hauling by train. "Door to door," that was the slogan. Mr. Hughes was going to change the way freight was moved in this country, and nothing less. During the war, he attracted a wealthy investor and traveled to the Palmer House Hotel in Chicago to seal the deal. However, they could not find manufacturing space—the story is vague again, hard to grasp—and the old man came back, states the son, "with his hat in his hand."

"He was fighting the freight system *and* the trucking system," says Roger. Years later, we are led to believe, the freight company Trailormobile offered Mr. Hughes $200,000 for his idea and he turned it down flat. It was worth millions, don't you know. He never made a penny from it. He slid from job to job.

"My father had the gift, just like I have the gift of gab," states Roger. But he does not say exactly what gift his father had. The gift, perhaps, of keeping a dream alive by holding out for all or nothing. By not letting it come true. But that kind of thinking did not work in Stalag 17. You had to take what you got. You had to adjust and adapt—keep the pain inside, sure, but not so much that it ate you alive. There was little opportunity in a POW camp for tilting at windmills, running at the wire, or sweet talking the Nazis. In the movies, yes. In real life, not so much.

So you walked the yard and played cards. Some guys dug collapsing tunnels. You read and reread your letters, if you were lucky enough to get them. Read the other guys', if you were not. You put up with a thousand aggravations and watched bones emerge against yellow skin as your weight flew away. You made do.

You waited.

He calls himself the "oddball." Unlike his brothers, Roger disliked homework and took every opportunity to ditch the house for a swim at the Boys Club. When he was old enough he would drive his mother to beano (bingo using beans as markers), then pick up a couple of friends and a couple of girls and just "fool away the time." In the spring of 1942 he met Mary and fell hard; wouldn't you know it, in August the draft board called. Roger chose the Air Corps.

"Not having any brains," says Roger, he could not settle for being an airplane mechanic. Not glamorous enough. So at the base in Miami he sweated off 30 pounds of pudge and earned his silver wings as a flight engineer. His training continued in the skies of the Pacific Northwest and by September of 1943 Roger's crew hop-scotched its plane to England to join the 94th Bomber Group.

Their first mission was the famous, long-distance raid on the hydroelectric dam at Rjuken, Norway. The facility churned out deuterium oxide, also known as heavy water, one of the key ingredients for making a nuclear bomb. Roger's squad also hit navy bases, factories in the suburbs of Paris, even a school for fighter pilots in Bordeaux, France. Under constant assault from fighter planes and exploding clouds of flak, the 94th lost crews at an alarming rate. The eleventh and final mission for Roger Hughes, on January 11, 1945, targeted factories south of Berlin and provided for him the ultimate lesson in adaptation. He became a bomb.

The plane was shot up. The bombs would not drop. Engines dying, systems failing. Roger descended from a turret with his walk-around bottle of oxygen and tried in vain to open the bomb-bay doors by hand. Then a cannon shell sliced through the plane, like a needle through fabric. The co-pilot, yelling "Let's go, let's go," accidentally opened his chute inside the plane and white silk whipped up everywhere. Chaos, pandemonium, men jumping away, and Roger got tossed violently against the bomb-bay doors. He passed out; the fuselage exploded; and he awakened some time in the very near future to find himself whole and hurtling through space.

He pulled the liner on his straggling chute and Roger the accidental bomb watched it blossom. His descent slowed. And now he was not heavy but light as a reed in the wind, and the wind, as it will, blew him according to its designs. The world passed fully out of Roger's control—and perhaps that

Roger Hughes as a young soldier.

had been the case all along, from the moment the Army summoned him to war—and when he collided with Germany, he looked up into the face of the local police chief holding a gun. And yet he was, miraculously, alive.

"I celebrate the day I was shot down," says Roger Hughes. "The whole damn German air force kicking the shit out of us and I walk away from it... you learn to count your blessings after awhile."

January 11th is for him a kind of birthday, the beginning of his second, bonus life. He will go out to dinner or at least raise a glass—it was a hell of a thing, what happened. One year he got together with his POW buddies at a hotel with a hot tub. No hot tubs at Stalag 17, that is for sure. After his retirement, Roger revisited the place in Germany where he fell to earth, where he was reborn, and then without remorse he traveled the long, hard road that followed from there, back in 1945.

First thing, he was paraded past civilians yelling "Luft gangster!" Then he was trucked to an air base and shipped overnight by passenger train to Frankfurt. After that, five days of misery standing in a fetid boxcar that shuddered to a stop at Stalag 17. How he endured that ride, Roger cannot really say. His memory has faded on it. He was but a speck in the war machine chewing the world.

The camp, what a dump. A tar paper village with a 48-seat outhouse stinking to heaven. The place was filthy and you could not get clean no matter what. And you could not be alone, except for tramping around for exercise. Later in 1944 the men cheered as Allied bombers slammed a nearby railroad yard and town. A bit of fun, letting off steam. "It was kind of stupid," says Roger. "The families of the guards lived down there." The POWs cheered anyway.

In the spring, the Germans closed the camp and force-marched the POWs for three weeks, away from the Russian onslaught. Roger came down with dysentery and fell behind in the column. "Why don't you shoot us and get it over with?" he demanded of the guards. But the rest of the memories are gone, somewhere he does not know. "All I remember," he says, "is we didn't have anything." Outside Brenau, in a pine forest on Easter Sunday, American tanks liberated the men and they were moved to an aluminum factory and then evacuated to rehab camps in France. Then, finally, they were shipped stateside, home.

At Fort Dix, Roger and other former POWs went through a chow line manned by German POWs, pink-cheeked healthy fellows in clean clothes, hair neatly shorn, their forearms muscled. They looked like anyone else and as they ladled food they spoke among themselves in whispered, incomprehensible German. The anger flared; the American boys could not keep it in any longer, could not let it slide. They gave those Nazi krieges some lip, all right.

"These guys, living in the lap of luxury," Roger states, and he sounds peeved about it now, 60 years later. Not that they should have been mistreated, but you have to understand, "there were days we weren't fed."

Roger took Mary for his wife, soon after the war. His father-in-law, a straight-up guy and World War I vet, made sure that he turned to the Veterans Administration for assistance. Roger received a 30 percent pension for extreme stress and weight loss due to imprisonment, and he took out a GI loan for a house down payment and used the Veteran's Preference law to land a job with the Postal Service.

Unlike his father, Roger Hughes never reached for the brass ring. He never dreamed of fame and riches, and he never wore the high, stiff collar or asked to be called anything but Roger, or Dad. He never tried to be more than he was, or ever could be. Flannel shirt and sneakers, good enough for him. Good enough just having a fine time with his beautiful wife and four children. And a night without dreams of falling like a bomb, of starving and wondering what you had done to deserve it, that was fine, too.

After the Postal Service, Roger ran a variety store with his brother-in-law for 14 years (they had the first soft ice cream machine in the area, he cannot

CRITICS ACCLAIM
"STALAG 17"
SEASON'S NEW
COMEDY SMASH!

"A TURBULENT AND GUSTY PLAY

Still shaking with the excitement of the performance . . . 'Stalag 17' is a stinging melodrama . . . Mr. Bevan and Mr. Trzcinski have made a turbulent and gusty play out of a haunting experience . . . Jose Ferrer has staged (it) with theatrical expertness . . . rowdy humor . . . racy and picturesque actors put on a flaring show."

—BROOKS ATKINSON, N. Y. Times

"ROCKED THE RAFTERS WITH YAKS!

Salty and authentic . . . frank and accurate . . . hilarious. Their characters are vivid and unbelievable, and their handling of situations is remarkable. Ferrer has cast the play with an admirable eye and staged it effectively. The customers enjoyed 'Stalag17.' They rocked the theatre rafters with their yaks, and stung their palms applauding."

—ROBERT COLEMAN, N. Y. Daily Mirror

WALTER WINCHELL IN NEW YORK

"A NEW HIT TITLED 'STALAG 17.' An entertaining Zipsy-Doodler with the Correct BANG-BANG tempo!"

"Towners are talking about the wizardry trouping in the 'Stalag 17' company."

"ANOTHER RECOMMENDATION

FOR 'STALAG 17,' is that the authors have been able to project the imaginative humor of the airmen without obscenities or blasphemy. The suspense is really melodramatic in intensity. An authentic contribution to the theatre."

—The Catholic World

"ONE OF THE BEST SHOWS OF THE SEASON! . . .

A forthright, exciting melodrama. It is tense and constantly interesting, it captures an emotional appeal that an audience should find pretty irresistible. José Ferrer, who is also the producer, has staged it with admirable skill and the all-male cast acts it for all the tingling suspense in it."

—RICHARD WATTS, JR., N. Y. Post

"AN EVENING FULL OF LAUGHS AND EXCITEMENT, TOO!

It is not often that theatregoers become so emotionally involved that, in the undoubting mood of children at a Punch and Judy show, they shout warnings to imperiled actors. Yet this is what happened at Mr. Bevan's and Mr. Trzcinski's premiere, and an exhilarating experience it was. The audience at 'Stalag 17' is no less a contributor to the fun, this is a proof of it."

—JOHN MASON BROWN, The Saturday Review

"A BOISTEROUS THRILLER!

A lively and theatrical show . . . seethes with a mixture of comedy and melodrama. These characters are brave, brash, and ingenious, and their dialogue is salty and slangy . . . A boisterous thriller." —OTIS GUERNSEY, N. Y. Herald Tribune

"UNQUESTIONABLY THE MOST ALL-OUT EXCITEMENT IN THE CURRENT THEATRE! HITS THE TOP!

Hits the top as gripping drama . . . The suspense grows close to unbearable . . . purest kind of vicarious thrills . . . rough and wild and persuasive . . . a fanfare of excitement . . . pure adventure . . . the play is beautifully staged by its producer, José Ferrer, so that every ounce of its excitement and compelling bewilderment comes to the surface. If it occurs to you that the setting of a prison camp during the war may be depressing, FORGET ALL SUCH NOTIONS. The authors . . . have presented here the most hilarious aspects of such a life. The humor is wry but it is rough and wild and persuasive too."

—WILLIAM HAWKINS, N. Y. World-Telegram & Sun

" 'STALAG 17' has The HOWLS of 'MISTER ROBERTS' and the HOORAYS of 'WHAT PRICE GLORY?' " —CUE MAGAZINE

In 1947, at the Shubert Theater in Boston, Roger Hughes and his wife attended this play loosely based on life at Stalag 17, where he was held captive. According to Roger, Senator John F. Kennedy sat a few rows behind him.

Roger Hughes

help crowing), but they lost their lease for convoluted reasons and then, incredibly, he became a guard at the Middlesex House of Corrections. "I was on the right side of the key," he says, winking. In truth, though, he could not help feeling sorry for the convicts. It is awful being locked away. When he could, he let the little infractions go.

Finally, Roger worked as a court bailiff for 20 years. The job paid well, but he did not enjoy the anguished proceedings, did not like witnessing everyone's troubles laid out like that. Most of all, the ambiguity bothered him. Nothing was straightforward or simple. Often there was no telling who was guilty and who was not—even after the verdict came down. And he wondered how the people on trial had gotten to these sad places in their lives. In many ways, he admits, the bailiff job was as bad as being a POW.

What did he do? He soldiered on, did his time. The money helped the kids through college. "It was something I put up with," Roger explains, because you cannot always fight the system. Sometimes you just have to adapt and adjust. You have to learn to count your blessings.

Look at this way: the whole goddamn German air force kicked the shit out of Roger Hughes and he walked away from it. And now his Tibetan terrier sleeps next to him on the couch, dreaming dog dreams in this house by the Cape Cod Canal.

CHAPTER 3

Kindness Endures, Love Redeems

CLINKERS: BOB COURNOYER'S STORY

If you could take an apple or a small potato, or a quick spoonful of sugar, you took it. Even if a rifle butt to the tailbone or base of the skull was your reward. Wire or cloth or wood was good for scavenging, too. "Anything you could get your hands on," says Bob Cournoyer, from Brockton, Massachusetts, held inside Nazi Germany as a prisoner of war from July 23, 1944 to April 19, 1945.

Once a scrap of wire came in handy as Bob and fellow POWs—Americans, Russians, French, and Poles—returned to their work kommando, a satellite of Stalag IVB, after another long day of digging potatoes in the fields of Erdeborn near the Czech border. The guards made them walk in the gutter, where the unworthy, the filth belonged. Sometimes passing civilians threw stones or yelled angry questions. Bob remembers an old man hitting him with a cane—he did not fault the man, his grief was so raw and undeniable. On this particular day, however, he saw a little girl scraping a broken wagon along the road. To hell with it, Bob told himself, and he left the gutter, hunched down, and used his wire to repair her wagon's faltering wheel. As she started away, he called out "Slow, slow," afraid that she would pull it along too quickly, with too much joy, and it would fall apart again.

Even though he lost 50 pounds, nearly one-third of his body weight, Bob survived his POW captivity on his feet and kicking. Luck, he says, that was it, and those spoonfuls of sugar he cadged while working in a nearby sugar beet processing plant after the harvest of '44. Luck was a scarce thing,

Bob Cournoyer

though. Some prisoners starved or were beaten to death by guards or just
lost hope. Sick men who stayed in their bunks in the morning were gone
for good when Bob returned in the evening, and no one knew what happened to them. So you got yourself up, got yourself going, no matter what.

At the sugar beet plant, he worked around the furnace with an old German man; the name is forgotten. He had a big white mustache and seemed
very tired. Mute to each other's language, they drew numbers in the dirt

with their fingers. Their ages, times of day, things like that. Sometimes the old man let Bob nap a bit and he did not object to his ever-ready sugar spoon. "I was in the right place, at the right time," Bob says. He had it pretty good there, at least compared to others.

One of his jobs was to take clinkers out of the furnace. Clinkers are lumps of coal fused into a vitrified, glassy substance. Fired hard as the hardest stone, they refuse to burn; left in the furnace, they gum up the works. With his bare hands Bob took out the clinkers and tossed them away. In slang a clinker means a blunder, but in the proper derisive context of an ass-backwards, black-is-white world, in which starving kids from Brockton work sugar beet fields under the German sun, it can also mean a triumph. A clinker, no matter what, will not be consumed.

Sometimes Bob was assigned to *arbietskommandos*, translated as "fatigue parties," to dig trenches for water and sewer pipes. You had to lay them six feet down to prevent freezing. It was punishing work, says Bob, and also "the only time I ever hit a German and got away with it." But barely—he struck a German civilian with a 50-pound sledgehammer, entirely by mistake, but that did not matter to the guard who pushed his gun into Bob's throat, ready to kill him, he's sure. The civilian yelled, "Nein, nein," and that saved his life. Dumb luck, really, getting past that one.

Deep in the winter of 1945, Bob was taken to the bombed-out town of Zietz, where for months he joined POWs chipping mortar off bricks in the freezing cold. His hands were exposed and his feet covered only in paper sandals (his boots had been confiscated and given to a German soldier). Again and again, the hammer slipped off the head of the chisel and pounded his gnarled left fist. As the ground rumbled with explosions and colossal armies ripped Germany to the bone, as the last days of the Third Reich neared, the POWs endlessly chipped mortar from brick. The cleaned-up bricks were to be used for rebuilding bread ovens. Thrifty and efficient to the last, the Germans. Bob's hands dripped blood into the snow at his feet and still he could not stop working, for there were always the guards and their rifle butts.

"If you broke the brick in the wrong spot, you'd get a whack in the back or the skull," says Bob. One guard, he remembers, swung his rifle like Ted Williams swung his baseball bat. "A couple of them, I could have chewed their necks off."

After the war, Bob was diagnosed with stomach ulcers and peripheral neuropathy in his hands and feet, a nerve disorder caused by vitamin deficiency and the intense labor he performed as a POW. (As compensation, the U.S. government gave him $1.50 for every day he was made to work for the Germans.) It was as if the nerves in his extremities were in revolt, as if they did not want to transmit the information they had dutifully collected. Today, after decades of treatment and surgeries, Bob's hands and feet continue to burn and itch or go numb and cold. He wears cotton gloves to bed and

The commandant of Bob Cournoyer's work kommando poses with his girl-
friend, or possibly wife, in front of the dance hall where POWs were housed.
The commandant gave this photo as a keepsake to Walter Hembrick, an
American POW, who later mailed a copy to Bob.

gets up in the middle of the night to douse his hands with hot water. There is
the PTSD, too, post traumatic stress disorder, and the nightmares and bad
day dreams that go with that.

Bob has never been one to lie down, though, not now and certainly not
after the war. For awhile he walked an outdoor route with the Postal Service, but had trouble handling small pieces of mail. So he learned to separate

letters by blowing gusts of air between them. It is amazing the simple things you take for granted, until your hands do not cooperate. Later he transferred indoors and worked as a postal clerk until his retirement in 1984. And like most vets, he sought the all-American life. This included marrying a beautiful girl named Eleanor whom he had admired in math class at Brockton High School. They had barely spoken in school, but that had not stopped Bob from jerry-rigging her safely into his prisoner's heart, from using her face and her smile to keep himself going in the sugar beet factory and the potato fields, in the bombed-out buildings of Zietz, and back at home they fell in love just as he had dreamed it. She gave him six children who in turn have given him 14 grandchildren and counting.

His Massachusetts license plate reads "EX POW 446" and is framed in red barbed wire. There is a perk to that: former prisoners of war are excused from paying excise tax on their cars. Another perk: the world sees that you exist. That you kept going.

Bob enjoys talking about certain aspects of his war. Take his first stint outside New England, at basic training in South Carolina. He was in high spirits and the drills seemed "fun, like in the backyard." Their instructors, veterans of the North Africa landings, warned the men to be serious and smarten up. But at least he knew enough to take his older brother Fred's advice and score badly in firing the machine gun, because those guys always get it, sooner or later.

He is equally enthusiastic about his combat experiences with the 90th Army Division. Bob went ashore at Utah Beach three days after the D-Day landings and remembers coming across dead cows laying in meadows, emitting "the first stink of death," an omen of what would come. His division fought for several weeks in Normandy and on the Cherbourg Peninsula, taking heavy casualties. The officers were green, the combat strategies unproven; one lieutenant sent his men through a break in a hedgerow and every last boy was shot down. And Bob absolutely loves telling the chocolate bar story, a complicated tale in which his refusal to share a Hershey bar even-Steven with a buddy sets off a chain of bloody, if not comical events.

He does not even seem to mind talking about his capture, when his unit was cut off on the "Island of Witches" in the Sieves River. They could not escape because the river swelled with rain; if only they had bypassed that godforsaken place, he laments, they could have joined Allied troops streaming through the breakout at St. Lo two days later. Instead, American officers ordered Bob and his mates to push their weapons into the mud and surrender to the Germans. So they obeyed their officers. Then they were lined up and marched out.

If one man escaped, a German guard announced, ten more would be shot. "We were scared to death," Bob remembers. "Will they shoot us down?" The Germans issued Bob his POW dog tags—number 50223. If he had died

Bob Cournoyer keeps this Luger pistol unloaded in a strong-box in his home. He personally confiscated it from a German officer when his work kommando was liberated by American troops.

in captivity, half of the dog tags would have been snapped off and sent to the Red Cross. "I still remember that number," says Bob. "I'll never forget it."

The story of his escape from captivity, during the chaotic end days of war in Europe, is also a pleasure for Bob to tell. He and a few mates crawled through a hole blasted in a roof—"pure luck," he admits, that a shell landed there—and hours later they returned, riding high on U.S. tanks, to liberate the camp and capture the men who had imprisoned them. One POW grabbed an M1 rifle and executed a guard who had been particularly sadistic. Bob, too, found a gun and ran to the command compound, where he confronted an officer dressed in a "beautiful coat" and boots polished to his knees. The man surrendered personally to Bob, and he took from him a 8mm Austrian-made Waffenfabkik Steyer, a heavy black pistol which he hid under his pillow at the 217th General Hospital in Paris, until alarmed nurses locked it away.

The gun now resides, unloaded, inside a strongbox next to a file cabinet. Nearby hangs a framed photo of Army buddies from basic training and a

Bob Cournoyer as a young soldier.

display case with his ribbons and medals. The Bronze Star is pinned there, awarded for his wild escape. There is also a three-paneled poster with photos and newspaper clippings about him—a triptych constructed by local school kids with "behavior problems," Bob states earnestly—and his old uniform resides on a hanger next to assorted clothes in exile. Sixty years of correspondence with the Department of Veterans Affairs is spread out in manila folders, for easy reference. All this, Bob's war, is kept in a tidy nook on the second floor landing that overlooks the living room of his condominium.

He speaks much more reluctantly about his days as a POW. Bob insists he will not return to Germany, where he "never had one goddamn good day," and he tells the story of a fellow ex-POW who went back to the German mine where he was used as slave labor. The trip was designed to "get it out of his system," but the poor guy came home more messed up than ever. So it is no wonder Bob is wary; no wonder he only livens up describing odd, cryptic moments that push back against his general tale of suffering.

Bob Cournoyer

On Christmas Eve, for instance, a crippled guard played *Silent Night* and *Lilly Marlene* on an old organ, while an American POW pumped the organ paddle for the German. It was "almost like he was one of us," says Bob. He remembers playing football with a rolled-up jacket, to the cheers of girls watching from outside the fence. They only did that once; it sapped too much energy. And there was the day he spied a soldier from his hometown across the sugar beet fields and yelled out, "Hey, Brockton" (Bob thinks the poor guy might have been shot escaping); and the way fuel tanks released from Allied planes bounced along the ground, making a ridiculous "boing, boing, boing" sound, followed by German civilians running out to scavenge fuel; and the time he looked out a window in the factory, while clearing away clinkers, and saw a little boy wave at him from the road with a bottle of milk in his hand.

He remembers that boy, vividly.

Then he tells the story of the little girl again, how he left the gutter to fix her wagon wheel and warned her, in a language she did not understand, "Slow, slow."

NEAR AND FAR: DON SIMPSON'S STORY

You were allowed one letter and one postcard per month. For the letter you received one sheet of tissue-thin paper that ripped if you pressed too hard. And when nothing came back, as the months passed, you wondered if your words were getting through, if they even knew you were alive back home.

Some guys let it get to them. Some were convinced they had been thrown over by girlfriends and even wives, given the old bum's rush when a home front sharpie came along. Just one more thing taken from you—first your gun, then your freedom, then your girl beyond the oceans.

But Don knew, he *knew* Mary cradled him in her thoughts. Penned in Stalag IIIC since September 1944, Don Simpson understood the pain she had to be feeling, as well as the grief of his mother who had lost three of six children as infants.

"I was very concerned about them," says Don, "that they were worrying themselves crazy." In his correspondence home he tried to be reassuring, set an upbeat tone without making it sound unbelievable. He certainly did not

Don Simpson

let on about the shrapnel wounds in his right hand and buttocks. Or that "the goddamned Germans" had taken Mary's class ring from him.

To his loved ones, Don was Missing-in-Action (meaning dead or POW) until notice of his capture came on the day before Christmas. The letters and cards he sent home began to arrive in January, but he did not know this. How could he? Mary's letters to him and the cigar bundles from his family bounced off Europe and landed back in the States.

Even so, even as other prisoners received mail, inhaling the words through fingers and eyes, even as one-third of his body weight disappeared—another loss, slow and aching—Don did not doubt. He knew that Mary was true. He knew that she was waiting for him.

They met in a pear tree. He was in the tree, actually, a 15-year-old kid picking pears for an elderly neighbor, and then she appeared on the sidewalk below. He called out to her, "Do you want a pear?" She stopped and replied, "Yes." It was not like him to do that, be so bold, and maybe he would not have said anything if they had passed each other walking, but he had a pear in his hand and the world seemed ripe with fabulous possibilities up in that tree.

She was 14 and wore a pretty dress. Her brunette hair hung to her shoulders, the way it did most of her life. Don tossed Mary a pear and she caught it, and he came down out of the tree with his own pear and they stood on the sidewalk and ate the fruit together. She lived up the street, he learned, just four houses away. He told her he was visiting his sister's family for the summer—and that was it for the boy, it was love at first sight in the faraway town of Hopkinton, Massachusetts. By and by, she continued on her way. He climbed back up the tree and finished picking the pears.

The next day, Don took a walk to the gas station for some penny candy. The route went past Mary's house, wouldn't you know, but she was nowhere to be seen. So he bought the candy and started on the sauntering return leg of his journey. This time she stood out front, hope made flesh, and Don gave Mary a handful of treats. He met her sister and brothers and the rest, he says, their life together, the next 66 years, just kind of happened from there.

"That's how it all opened up," Don says. They did not really date that summer, but he found a million excuses to hang around, and for her part she let him drive her father's 1930 Ford truck on dirt roads through the woods. When he returned to Waynesburg, Pennsylvania, for his sophomore year, Don and Mary began writing each other—short letters, two or three times a week—and the following summer he returned to his sister's house near the old thread mill, and he kissed her.

Following his junior year, Don dropped out of high school and joined the Army, even though he was only 17 years old. His parents agreed to sign the permission papers, but his sister protested angrily. What's the hurry getting yourself killed? Mary was not happy about it, either. Of course it was late

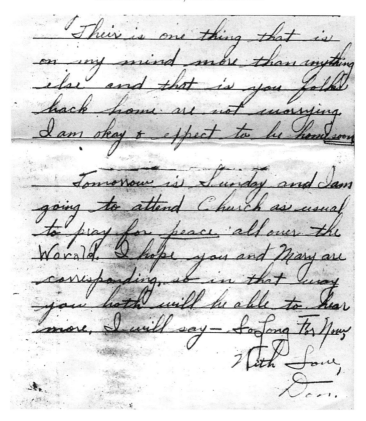

Don Simpson never received any mail in Stalag IIIC, but he sent many letters home. In this excerpt from a *kriegsgefangenenpost* to his parents, a starving and wounded Don attempts to soothe their feelings.

1942 and you did not stay behind if you could help it. The map of Europe was drenched in Nazi black, Asia in Jap red, and besides most of his buddies were already in. So Don and Mary exchanged their class rings, each with a blue stone set into it, and he departed for basic training in Virginia.

After basic, Don got tagged for the 145th Combat Engineers to learn about mines and booby traps and Bailey Bridges. What a stroke of luck, in the summer of '43! He was assigned to New York City to study DC generators and wasn't that the high life—sleeping in a hotel, riding the subways near and far, and cheering the Brooklyn Dodgers at Ebbets Field. Everything was free for servicemen: shows, restaurant meals, cigarettes, "and boy did I take advantage of it," Don says. Best of all, he was close enough to take weekend passes to Hopkinton. This broke the rule against going more than 50 miles from your post. A military policeman snared him once, remembers Don, but the guy let him go after getting an earful about beautiful Mary.

The luck did not hold. Don's unit shipped to Alaska and then Oregon—on one furlough, he rode for two weeks on cross-country trains to spend one week with Mary—and then finally back to New York City for embarkation in April 1944. He recalls the long ride from Oregon on a World War I-era train, the coal-powered engine shooting cinders that blackened the windows and blew into the cars, settling on the soldiers sleeping upright in their seats. You had to keep knocking the ash off your face and uniform. Don and Mary had decided not to marry before he went abroad, mostly because he did not want to leave her with a child who might never know his father.

Because it took a German sub about ten minutes to line up a boat, the troop transport USS *Mariposa* changed course every nine minutes. Don slept in a hammock on a heaving deck. When they arrived at the village of Altringham, England, his battalion practiced bulldozing hedgerows and assembling Bailey bridges at night—a delicate engineering feat, remarks Don, a real lesson in counterbalancing. They visited the pubs and waited for the word. On D-Day Plus One, the 145th Combat Engineers hit Omaha Beach.

"We lost a lot guys," says Don. A fact, and he says nothing more of it. In the months ahead, he fought in several battles, "zooming across France with old blood-and-guts Patton," as much a grunt with a gun as an engineer. The quirky details still amaze him, how troops signaled back and forth with little clickers to avoid shooting each other, and how Allied planes dropped aluminum foil over St. Lo to disrupt radio transmission. There were dead, stinking cows everywhere. Don recalls digging a giant hole with a Bobcat and watching the 'dozers push the carcasses down into it.

Their advance stopped at Nanci, France. Don blames Eisenhower; he should have let Patton, "a dedicated warmonger," go all the way to Germany. Maybe then the Battle of the Bulge never would have happened. And maybe Don never would have been captured, on September 4, 1944, if Ike had just let Patton stick in the spear.

They were putting up a Bailey after midnight, over a canal. Don, a platoon sergeant, took a few men upstream and crossed over in a boat, then came back downstream to where the bridge would meet the far shore. "That was the end of me," he says. A squad of Germans ambushed them, Don got shot in the ass and wrist, and then "they beat the hell out of us."

After interrogation, he found himself in a column of POWs on a long march through Luxemburg. The men were allowed to pick from apple trees along the road, an act that was forbidden the moment they crossed into Germany. Those apples grew for Germans and no one else. Better they rot than go in the wrong stomach. A four-day boxcar ride in filthy, crowded conditions took Don to Stalag IIIC, east of Berlin on the Polish border, where he spent the next five months.

An English doctor dug shrapnel from Don and sprinkled white powder in the wounds. That was some magic powder—the wounds did not get

Don Simpson as a young soldier.

infected. As winter descended and Don turned 20 in the camp, as no word
arrived for him week after week after week, he found himself feeling sorry
for the older POWs. The men with wives and children appeared especially
distraught. Don could imagine what they were thinking. He already considered Mary his wife, documents or not. Their future, their life in Hopkinton,
it was all there inside him. He could see their beautiful children as plain as
day; he could hear them laughing, and playing, and climbing trees.

At Stalag IIIC, the best you could do was walk the yard and try not to lose
your cool. The men subsisted on rutabaga or potato soup, and they passed
hours playing pinochle. Time dragged, drawing out the hunger so much that
"you'd see a bird," says Don, flying free over the camp, "and you'd say, if I
could just get my hands on that bird, I'd eat it in one gulp."

The POWs were made to pull carts of rutabagas and potatoes to the kitchen. One day Don witnessed an Italian POW snatch "one lousy potato" and a young guard shot him dead for it, right there, at close range. Later that winter the young guards were sent to die on the eastern front and replaced by older ones, some in their seventies. In the end, every last guard in camp was lined up and executed when the Russians liberated the camp in February.

They came in Lend-Lease Sherman tanks; they rode in like cowboys in Ford trucks. Many of the drivers were women "who looked more like guys than most guys," laughs Don. He remembers the Russian soldiers as crude and wild and uneducated, but he does not fault them for that, they could not help how they were raised. You get the cards you're dealt and you play them the best you can. Go to Odessa, the Russians told the POWs, and then roared out of camp.

"Where the hell is Odessa?" asked Don.

Odessa, the Black Sea port, was on the way home to Mary. Better than mail, he would send himself! Don and a few friends teamed with a soldier named Joe who spoke Armenian and scraps of Russian, and they headed south by southeast across Poland. They were, says Don, "delighted to be out," and Polish families often invited them inside for hot meals and a soft bed. There was one tight spot: Russian soldiers almost shot them for being Austrians, but Joe talked their way out of it.

After three weeks, the former POWs passed into the Ukraine and boarded a train for Odessa. There they were picked up by Russian police, deloused by a gang of rough female guards, packed on an American liberty ship, and shipped west by way of Constantinople, Port Said, and Naples. Don managed a phone call to Mary to tell her he was okay. As spring bloomed he entered the port of Boston, among the first group of POWs returned from either theater of World War II.

But they would not let him off the ship. Twenty-five miles away and "I couldn't see my girl," he says. "I couldn't see Mary." The men were sent to Camp Miles Standish for processing—an Army specialty, processing. Finally, days later, Don shook himself free and took a train to South Station in Boston, then transferred to another train going west to Framingham. He remembers stepping onto the platform, where Mary had arranged to meet him.

All around, GIs were reuniting with their families. Everywhere, hugs and happy voices. Don scanned the platform. Then he saw her. Mary stood apart, at a distance, wearing a beautiful hat. They saw each other and—it might sound sappy, but it is true—she ran across the platform to her Don, into his arms, and they held each other and cried.

Now he pauses in the telling, appearing a bit startled as if the memory had taken form before him. Quite a welcome, he says. And then, boy, did they blow some dough, living it up in New York City! All his back pay! Mary and Don saw the sights, rode the trolleys, and danced to the big bands like it was the end of the world. You cannot imagine how that felt.

And they discovered this: they were each changed, each tougher, but their love had not diminished. Forty million killed, but for them the war had been nothing more than an interruption of events that were meant to happen from the day Don tossed Mary her pear and she caught it, just like that.

They married and moved to Baltimore, where his parents now lived. He finished high school and earned a degree in engineering from the University of Maryland. The young couple returned to Hopkinton and eventually bought a house not far from their pear tree, and they raised two children who are raising three grandchildren. For decades Don worked as an engineer for Dennison Manufacturing Co., maker of crepe paper, gummed paper labels, and paper dolls. When the kids moved out, Don and Mary traveled—how they loved to travel—to Hawaii and the Caribbean and all over the United States (but never to Europe, enough of that).

Mary died in August of 2001, after suffering for years from amyotrophic lateral sclerosis (ALS), also known as Lou Gehrig's disease. The disease, which erodes nerve connections between the brain and the muscles, began for Mary with numb feet and hands and ended with her struggling for breath. Her mind stayed sharp throughout, doggedly trying to make contact with her body, to move her limbs, to touch her husband. The remaining class ring—the one he gave her to keep in 1942—has passed to their daughter Marsha.

Don Simpson, at 80, looks several years younger than his age, even though he suffers from emphysema. His hair is thick and black, combed back like it was 1945. The house is impeccably clean and fashioned with a hundred feminine touches—Mary's touches, undisturbed. Yet Don is not trapped here, in a museum of the way it was. He has kept up the traveling. "I just got my driver's license renewed for five more years," he says proudly.

It is the same trip, every April. Don gets in the car and drives south, visiting relatives at every stop along the way: niece in Baltimore, great niece in Virginia, nephew in Georgia, nephew in the Panhandle of Florida (a doctor, they go fishing together), nephew in Sarasota, cousin in Houston, and a whole batch of family in Kansas. And then home to Hopkinton, into the fullness of spring.

The 5,500-mile journey takes six weeks, if all goes well. When Don heads out in April 2005, it will be the fourth time he has traveled the route. His Mercury Grand Marquis waits in the garage, on this cold January day, equipped with everything a veteran traveler needs: power steering, cruise control, sun roof, you name it. Driving long distances is not a chore for him. He knows how to relax behind the wheel, one hand casually draped at twelve o'clock. He knows how to enjoy the world as it streams by.

"It's the freedom, the joy of seeing new things," he says. "How thankful I am that I live in such a wonderful country, where I can do such things."

Don Simpson

As he drives, Don listens to tapes of the 1940s big bands. Artie Shaw, Glenn Miller—all the great ones that he and Mary danced to when they were young, when he came home from the war in one piece and there she was waiting for him, so lovely, on the train platform. On the rolling, open road, it all comes back to him like it was yesterday.

Don Simpson never took his southern ramble in the spring of 2005. His emphysema worsened and later that year he suffered a stroke. Don moved to a nursing home and died in the summer of 2006.

UNKNOWN CONSEQUENCES: BOB NOBLE'S STORY

When Gloria married Bob, she accepted that her husband would not talk about his war experiences. People don't want to hear a bunch of old stories, he said, but she knew he felt that being a POW was nothing to be proud of—or worse. "Why didn't you run?" she remembers a friend asking Bob, about his capture.

Besides, it was hard to explain the way things happened.

The 18-year-old kid heard someone speaking German in the dark and wondered, Hey, who's fooling around? He poked his head up from his slit trench dug on the top of a hill in Alsace-Lorraine, a region disputed for centuries and now under Nazi control, and he spied a group of men standing together maybe ten yards away. It was hard to make them out, gray figures in the black. More German sounds traversed the cold air and Bob Noble hoisted his rifle into firing position.

"A lot of things happened because of decisions that I made," Bob says now, "and I don't know why I made some of them." He has been married 56 years to Gloria and boasts a son and three daughters, ten grandchildren, and two great-grandkids (tonight they will hear one of them sing in a choir). Framed photos of children through the ages knit the walls of their condo, but the very existence of those children hung fire that night in the slit trench as Bob leveled his gun at the huddle of ghost-men. The sounds of a dread language choked his ears.

He did not shoot. He heard a voice in his head: "Don't do this." Bob lowered the gun. The men he had picked out for death, in fact, were American GIs who had just been captured by Germans infiltrating their position from the rear. Moments later Bob was captured, too. It was December 16, 1944, and the Battle of the Bulge had begun 90 miles to the north.

"I've thought about it a lot," says Bob, of the events that led to his capture, to misery, and to survival. To Gloria, to Boston College on the GI Bill, to a career as an engineer at a screw machine company. To this morning, lounging in gray sweats and running sneakers. "You make a decision," he says, "but you don't know the consequences."

The new POWs were forced to carry injured German soldiers, cradled in blankets. They were marched east and kept in a barn on top of the Siegfried Line, dating from World War I—the last war, the Great War. American artillery started up, ceaselessly, and one shell caved in a wall not ten feet from Bob. "It was like a dream," he remembers, standing in the shoes of

Bob Noble

the enemy. They followed their guards down a stairway into a blast-proof room. In the morning, the POWs were marched out of town—Bob is not sure what town—while it burned, while the American shells continued to fall without ever asking, friend or foe?

At a transit camp in Lansdule, he turned 19 years old. The POWs slept in a hut with a collapsed floor that admitted biting winter winds, and they had no bunks and no blankets. A few men staged an escape but were brought back the next day. The guards let it be known: two would be shot for each one that tried to escape. They lived by another equation: one small loaf of black rye bread shared every day by four men.

That Christmas Eve, Bob and his fellow POWs made candles with snips of string and waterproof dubbing. Protestant, Catholic, Jewish, they read from prayer books and sang Christmas carols. Bob had trained with some of the men—the men of the 87th Division, the Golden Acorns, who had ferried up the Hudson River in September of '44, boarded the *Queen Elizabeth* with 15,000 other troops, outrun German Sea Wolf submarines, and put into the Firth of Clyde where they jumped from cargo nets into landing crafts with 70 pounds on their backs. The same grunts who went ashore at Le Havre, France, who joined Patton's Third Army, who besieged the fortress at Metz. Now they read prayers and sang their favorite holiday songs.

"We were alive and together," remembers Bob. "It was a special feeling that I haven't had since."

It was Christmas, too, in Dorchester, Massachusetts, and his parents longed to hear from their boy. They knew his unit had landed in France, and that was all. New Year's passed without a letter. Then on January 5, 1945, a Western Union telegram arrived from an official in the War Department. "The Secretary of War desires me to express," it read, the black ink

Bob engraved this prison camp spoon with his name and date of capture—"12/17/44." He whittled the wooden paddles for mixing powdered milk and coffee with snow, and to pass the time.

spreading across the borders of the blocky letters, typed large on flimsy paper, "his deep regret that your son has been reported missing in action..."

Across town, Gloria had been attending Wednesday night novenas at Saint Ambrose's. It was, to be honest, the only way she could get out of the house. Her parents could not likely bar her from church! At the novenas she remembers hearing the Father say, "These flowers have been donated by the family of Robert G. Noble, Missing-in-Action." New flowers arrived week after week, placed next to the altar, and the Father spoke the same words again and again. As winter deepened, Gloria kneeled in church and began to wonder, Who is he? Who is Robert G. Noble, Missing-in-Action? Will he ever return from the land of the missing? She joined in the prayers for him.

Bob, meanwhile, was forced to dig trenches for antiaircraft emplacements, even as American P-47s hit nearby rail yards. The ground was frozen a foot and a half deep, hard as iron against the picks and shovels they swung

Bob Noble as a young soldier.

with their bare hands. One day the P-47s strafed their field and the POWs dove into a trench. Bob, slowed by frostbit feet, landed on top of the pile. He looked up and saw gun-flashes on the wings of the planes. The bullets came close, but for some reason passed him by.

In the following weeks his frostbite worsened, requiring him to stay behind when his group was marched out of camp. Later he learned that those men endured a terrible ordeal on the march, with many deaths, and he is not sure that he would have survived if he had gone along. He was, he supposes, lucky.

But not so lucky to avoid a shuttling, four-day train ride to Stalag 5A in Ludwigsburg. Guards crammed Bob and 120 men in a single boxcar. Less than half could sit at any one time, so they alternated up and down. Up was better, actually, since Bob had "no meat left on my buttocks." The POWs were barely fed and let out of the boxcar only once. They relieved themselves in their helmets, which they pitched out an opening in the rear of the moving train. Some of them became agitated—"We're Americans, they can't do this to us!"—but Bob was determined to roll with the punches. Getting mad just didn't help.

At 5A, the ratio of POW per loaf of bread soared to 8:1, and as weeks passed Bob's weight fell drastically (he emerged from captivity 100 pounds dripping). Complaining of stomach pains got him sent to a building staffed by British doctors captured at Arnheim. "Did I really feel sick?" asks Bob. He shakes his head. "I took advantage of the opportunity that presented itself." Returning three days later, once more his bunkmates had been marched away. It was almost as if his absence had triggered it; the cause and effect, like everything, was all screwed up. "One of those decisions," Bob says without affect. He does not know what happened to the men who disappeared, except that a buddy named Fleming died at another camp.

Back home at Saint Ambrose's, new flowers continued to grace the altar, and the very same words, "...donated by the family of Robert G. Noble, Missing-in-Action," floated down the rows of pews. Kneeling Gloria heard and wondered.

Then word came...nothing definitive, but something. A ham radio operator named Sanford Lowe in Richmond, Washington, sent a postcard to Bob's parents reporting a message he heard from their son in a German propaganda broadcast. It was true; Bob had been pulled from the line at the Marlag Nord interrogation center and told to speak into a wire recorder. He let the folks at home know he was alive, but he is pretty sure that he did not say "we are treated well," as the postcard claimed. The War Department routinely told distraught families not to put much stock in second-hand reports grabbed by amateurs from airwave static.

On April 12, 1945, President Franklin D. Roosevelt departed this world. On April 15, the clouds around Stalag 5A glowed from searchlights and the POWs broke into *God Bless America*, which ticked off the Germans.

And on the morning of the sixteenth, the guard tower stood empty as British tanks popped up like mushrooms on the ridge above the camp. The POWs washed in a nearby stream, ate cans of Bully Beef—"awful stuff," winces Bob—and waited for evacuation. A reporter for the *Chicago Tribune* wrote down the names of the American POWs.

A few days later, Bob's mother attended a wake. His father, home ill, answered the phone and spoke with a newspaper reporter. Immediately he dialed the funeral home and asked for his wife. At the news she shrieked so loudly, the story goes, that the corpse sat up in its coffin, and the wake died right there and became a party for the life and liberation of her son, homeward bound.

The day after *that*, Bob's parents received a Red Cross postcard that he had filled out in January, officially verifying his status as a POW.

Following two weeks at an English hospital, and an ocean voyage, Bob strolled down Commonwealth Avenue in Boston to Army headquarters. There he was debriefed and advised, sternly, to remain quiet about his experiences. Keep your lip zipped; play it close to the vest. It was the same line for most POWs. But not even the Army could stop him from cutting loose.

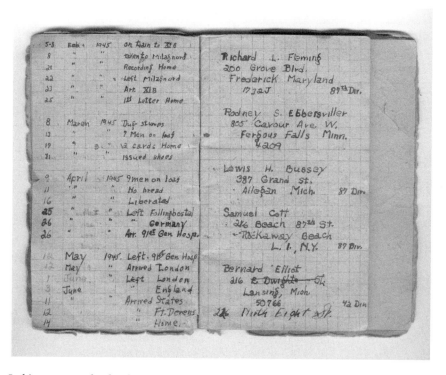

In his camp *taschenbuch,* or "pocket book," Bob recorded daily logs and the home addresses of fellow POWs.

In August, Bob took the "52/20" discharge: 20 bucks a week for 52 weeks. He borrowed his dad's Buick LaSalle and became a ferryman to the dance halls—Nutting's on the Charles, the Meadows, the Riverview Ballroom, the Totem Pole. He danced with a thousand girls and swung to the big bands of Vaughn Monroe and Harry James. Just about every night he cut loose, and who could blame him?

On one of those summer nights, it happened that Gloria noticed Bob and thought to herself, what a funny looking boy! She asked around—the scrawny kid with the big ears, who is he? None other, to her amazement, than Robert G. Noble, Missing-in-Action. The mysterious boy of the flowers, who floated on Wednesday night prayers. And yet here he was—not missing. Not dead. Not words, but flesh.

His father died of lung cancer in 1948, disappointed, Bob believes, never to have heard his son's war stories. It was not until the 1980s that he opened up. A psychologist at the Veterans Administration helped Bob realize that he had nothing to be ashamed of, no matter what anyone said. His experiences, he learned, should not be cocooned in silence.

"They were not treated with dignity," says Gloria.

Gradually, Bob has become more comfortable talking about his capture, the camps, almost everything. He has gone to ex-POW conventions, with Gloria by his side, and he even gave a speech on POW/MIA Recognition Day, on the deck of the USS *Massachusetts*. It is all a matter of confidence, he says. "I have more to say than I ever had before." In 2004, Bob traveled to the opening of the World War II Memorial in Washington, DC, and he was treated like gold, like solid gold. Former POWs were given red, white, and blue boutonnieres to wear on their jacket lapels. They met senators and spoke to the media. Regular folks shook Bob's hand and thanked him. It was, in some ways, a homecoming long delayed.

Robert G. Noble, Missing-in-Action, knows in his bones that he did his duty. He made decisions, like any soldier, like any person, and they turned out the way they did.

THE GOOD GERMAN: LOUIS TARANTINO'S STORY

Other former POWs have said to him, "How can you be so nice to a German?" Louis understands their anger, their hurt, but he also knows what he knows and from that there is no backing down.

"That guy was good to me," he says. "He made me feel comfortable, his kindness helped." Christian Moritz, age 17, former Hitler Youth and prison guard at a work kommando in the cruel winter of 1945, treated American POW Louis Tarantino like a human being.

It was the little things, which were everything. Now and then Christian gave Louis an extra half-slice of bread, or a little more barley soup. In the frostbiting cold, on ditch-digging details, he let Louis pause and stuff his bare hands in his pockets. Christian spoke some English; Louis had picked up a little German. They talked about sports and movies and their families. Louis told stories about his job at a shoe store, about the secrets of selling to women. Someday, Christian confided, he would become a school teacher in his hometown of Meerane. And wouldn't you know it, he was crazy for all things American.

They got along like two men who were not enemies.

How did it start? Louis is not sure, but it was probably because he paid the boy a little attention. Some of the POWs, you could not talk to them they were so bitter at the world. None of that with Louis—it was not in his nature to clam up. So he made small talk with Christian and it turned out the kid was "a peach," says Louis, a nice, family boy with a faraway, dreamy air about him. It was almost like he was doing time, too. And he could be a regular comedian. One time Christian asked Louis to hold his rifle, then raised his hands and yelled, "Don't shoot!"

In the final days, Christian somehow avoided the Battle of Berlin, the conflagration that consumed German boys by the tens of thousands. From the U.S., Louis and his wife Louise sent him care packages with food and cigarettes, anything he might need. But Christian was stuck in the eastern

Louis Tarantino

occupation zone, controlled by the Russians. Soon the iron curtain slammed down and there was nothing but silence from his end.

In fact, states Louis, Christian Moritz was not the only good German he came across. Others helped him out, too. The old woman at the train station, for instance. She took a big risk to offer a small kindness.

One remarkable thing about Louis Tarantino is that he looks, at 81 years old, a lot like he did when he was 20 and presented himself to the draft board in Brockton, Massachusetts. Some old men contain only rough echoes of their former selves, perhaps in the eyes or the set of the chin, the drain of years having transformed their faces nearly beyond recognition. The old Louis, however, is basically a weathered version of the young Louis, his black, comb-backed hair now gray and comb-backed. His skin is wrinkled and a bit mottled, of course, but youth blushes close to the surface, almost as if he was a young actor made up to play his elderly self.

Indeed, to the stranger's eye, there are no traces of the triple-bypass—a "valve job" on his heart, he calls it—that he underwent in the summer of 2004. The operation almost killed him. It took a second operation, actually, just minutes after the first, to wrangle a stubborn bleeder. That, he likes to say, was close shave #3.

People know Louis from decades ago. A shoe salesman all his life, women will stop him in the grocery store and say, "I know you. You sold me a pair of pumps in 1958, for my sister's wedding." That kind of thing gets Louise's eyes rolling. Her husband, a natural salesman, likes people and they like him back. They do not have to live with the whole package, though. "He can be a pain in the neck," she says, but in a tone that converts the words into, "I love you." Because Louis is hard of hearing, she speaks loudly and modulates her voice according to his reactions.

He was the barber's only son; everyone hailed him around the neighborhood. Antonio Tarantino, an immigrant from the village of Canosa di Pulgia in Italy, cut hair at the end of Hanover Street in Boston's North End, in a ground-level shop that was eventually torn down to make way for a tunnel to the airport. After school, Louis swept clippings off the floor while Papa cut men's hair, plus a few "boy's bobs" for the young ladies. It was some joint, nine chairs and still waiting. A haircut cost a quarter.

When he had pushed enough hair around, Papa might give Louis a dime for the movies, enough for two tickets and candy at the Gem. He loved the Tom Mix cowboy pictures and serials like *The Perils of Pauline*, each chapter ending with the terrified heroine tied to the railroad tracks, hanging from a cliff, quivering inches from death at the nod of a villain.

Pauline always survived. Louis's mother had not, victim of heart disease when he was seven. He does not remember much about the funeral, it is such a blur. The wake was held at the house, he is sure of that, and he recalls "a thousand coats on the bed," mounded like he had never seen before. All those coats for Mama. A few years later, Louis and his sister gained a step

Infantryman Louis Tarantino hung these images of Christ and the
Cross around his neck. They are encased in rubber peeled from a gas
mask, in order to keep them from making noise on night patrols.
Guards in Louis's POW camp stripped the prisoners of jewelry, but
let him keep these icons.

family when Antonio married a widow from the old country with three
daughters. Big changes, but Louis stayed the heir and favored one.

In the late 1930s, as events accelerated to war in Europe and the Pacific,
he dreamed of joining the Navy. Swimming and fishing on Cape Cod had
made him crazy for sea water. Papa, though, was dead set against it. Then
the Japanese attacked Pearl Harbor and Louis rushed to enlist. To his great
distress, and Papa's joy, he was rejected for a hernia no one had even known
about—a gift, or a curse, from above. Louis kept his job at Izzy Cohen's
shoe store in Brockton, a working-class town south of Boston. It was
1942, though, and his friends were in the service: "Walking down the street,
it's all females, and you knew you're alone." After much pleading he

convinced his parents to pay for a hernia operation, and as soon as it healed he signed up for the infantry.

"I decided I'd rather die on land than in the water," says Louis. "If you've got your feet on the ground, you have a shot. On the ocean you've got the deck, and once that's gone, you're done."

He loved being a grunt. First up, basic training at Camp Blanding, Florida. Next, antitank training at Fort Meade, Maryland. "It made you feel great, like you accomplished something—some guys think that's crazy. I was in top condition, a dynamo at 140 pounds." In the POW camps, it was the big, heavy men who had the hardest time. As soon as they lost 15 or 20 pounds, he says, they became weak as kittens.

In September of 1944, Louis and his division of "replacements" shipped out of New York Harbor on the RMS *Aquitania,* an ocean liner converted into a troop ship. At the same time, in Germany, Christian Moritz was surely dreaming of doing the reverse. New York City was his obsession, Louis remembers. Christian wanted to sail into the harbor, behold the Statue of Liberty, and climb the Empire State Building. He wanted to watch American baseball players hit stupendous home runs. He wanted to set off for California and see the movies made in Hollywood.

On December 16, 1945, Louis and his company were inserted into a thin line of troops assaulted by SS Panzer divisions on the French-German border. The Americans' 12-pound artillery shells barely dented the Nazi Tiger tanks. Three days into the Battle of the Bulge, the lieutenant ordered a retreat into the snowy Ardennes Forest. Freezing and out of ammunition, wandering under a sunless gray sky, Louis's company dismantled their weapons and walked, hands up, toward German troops.

Louis, however, had forgotten about the big trench knife on his belt. A young SS trooper approached him and cocked his gun. They stood just feet apart, staring at each other. Then, as if someone was watching over him, a German officer convinced the storm trooper not to fire. That was close shave #1. Not far away in Malmedy, hundreds of captured Americans were slaughtered that week.

Louis and his company were marched overland, loaded on boxcars, and sent on an excruciating ten-day trip to the eastern edge of Germany. Ten days, says Louis, stopping his tale. He had never considered how many events took ten days. Ten days shoving off at Camp Standish, ten days on the *Aquitania,* ten days bivouacked in Scotland, ten days in the awful boxcar, smashed together and hungry. His young face turns older and reddens more, his eyes mist over, and he fumbles with his papers and maps. Ten days—a quirky detail, but jarring and unwelcome. It's too late in the game for new and perplexing mysteries. He has spent too many years making sense of the damn thing to have to grapple with this, the meaning of ten.

All told, 6,000–7,000 Americans were captured in the first week of the Bulge. Louis was dumped at Stalag 4B in Wittenburg, a camp filled with

Christian Moritz, a man Louis called a "good German," on the streets of Meerane in East Germany after the war. On the back of the photo, Christian wrote, "Your German friend, Christian, March 1949."

Englishmen, Italians, French, and Russians, and then put to work at a local brick factory, for zero dollars an hour. (Uncle Sam sent Louis 122 bucks after the war for his POW labor, saying it was from the German government. "A load of baloney," he says.) Close shave #2 took place at the brick factory.

He was cold, always cold, so Louis snuck into the boiler room for a bit of heat. He placed his wet gloves on the boiler but left them there, a stupid thing to do, and they burnt to a crisp. As he left the boiler room, a guard saw him and rushed forward with his rifle in firing position. Saboteur! They found the charred gloves—saboteur! Then more guards arrived and they argued among themselves. Shoot him! Nein, nein, let him go. The guards were younger than Louis, just kids, and not particularly well fed, either. Finally they decided to let him go.

"They weren't all Nazis," Louis says. "Some Germans were good."

Like the old woman at the train station. Louis and three other POWs, in transit from a work detail, stood on the platform during a bombing raid. The old woman ran a little canteen with donuts and coffee and soup. She and Louis made eye contact and then, after checking that the guards were distracted, she slid a bowl of soup across her counter to Louis. He drank it down, so delicious, and slid the bowl back. She could have been shot for helping an enemy of the Reich.

In mid-January, Louis was transferred to a work kommando where he spent three months digging ditches and building roadblocks around a small town, a vain measure to stop the Russians. That is where he met Christian

Louis Tarantino as a young soldier.

Louis Tarantino

and where his weight slipped from 140 to 98 pounds and would have sunk lower if not for the extra bread and soup from his friend.

Around the same time, Antonio Tarantino received a telegram from the War Department, informing him that his beloved son was Missing-in-Action. He assumed the worst and became, Louis was told, "like a zombie, worthless to anyone." Only after Louis was liberated that spring by the

Russians did his father learn that he had been a POW. But those Russians, says Louis, they were worse than the Germans. On horseback, they walked the POWs around Germany for two weeks, giving them little to eat, and the men heard rumors of trains filled with Allied prisoners leaving for Siberia. Finally Louis and a few buddies got so fed up they broke for it and ran bang into American troops at the Elbe River. It was over. At camp Lucky Strike, where POWs recuperated, Louis spooned himself so much sugary preserves that his lips swelled twice their size.

He came home and took up selling shoes again, his profession until retirement. "I was the best," he says. Louis married Louise, a girl who worked at his aunt's dry goods store, and they had two children. But Christian was not forgotten. The Tarantinos' care packages sailed out, back to the land of Louis's incarceration, and nothing came back.

In 1990, when the Berlin Wall fell, a box arrived. It was covered with funny-looking airmail stamps. Inside were a set of silver espresso spoons and a thank you letter, from Christian Moritz, for the very kind supplies sent over 40 years ago. Sorry for the delay, he wrote.

Since that time, Louis and Christian have exchanged letters, translated by Christian's son. They have had halting conversations on the phone. But they have never met again. Louis visits Italy but will not make the trip to Germany—it is too far, he says—and for all his longing, Christian has never come to America and set eyes on the Empire State Building. His wife's illness keeps him home, he says.

Maybe it is just as well. Maybe their memories are enough.

CHAPTER 4

You Are Not Forgotten: American POWs and the Search for Healing

You cannot easily read an old man from his face. A weathered and grooved landscape, it is formed from inside and out, by time and experience. It can seem unreal, even, like a mask grown over a subtler surface. The world is too dense and scrabbled upon it, and that is why an old man's face both lures and repels younger eyes.

The men who fought World War II are old now. Because of their unique and troubling experiences, the faces of former POWs of that war, rendered starkly in this book's photographs, often disguise more than they reveal. These faces share a kind of stubborn wariness on the verge between sadness and bravado—an expression common, perhaps, to the mid-twentieth century American man. Yet something unspoken and raw and sad roils beneath the well-worn lines and deep shadows.

It would be a mistake to underestimate the psychic injury incurred by the POWs of WW II, who were denied the public absolution that prisoners from more recent wars have, increasingly, been given. As the stories here indicate, POWs suffered guilt and humiliation for their capture and captivity, and to varying degrees have continued to be plagued by those feelings. Some chose not to talk; others were told by superiors in the military and government officials to button their lips. During their discharges, a number of former POWs were motivated into signing—as in, sign it or you are not leaving this man's army—a "Security Certificate for Ex-Prisoners of War."

Prepared by Military Intelligence Service, the document enjoined ex-POWs to keep their activities during captivity "SECRET" not only for "the duration of the war against the present enemies of the United States

POW license plate

but in peace-time as well." The stated reason was to avoid publicity that could, by a vague kind of logic, imperil American POWs still held in Japanese camps as well as "American prisoners in the event of future wars."

The consequences of silencing former POWs were devastating for them, according to Charles Walsh, a licensed counselor with the Department of Veterans Affairs. "It prevented them from seeking treatment for many years to come, and it effectively denied that there were long-lasting effects from being a POW."

The overarching message: No one wants to hear it. Buck up and go about your business, soldier. And they did.

They returned home determined to make up for what they missed, to take nothing for granted. By and large, they came from poor families and were not even thinking of college. Some of the airmen, who had soared at 25,000 feet over Fortress Europe, did not know how to drive a car. Some had best gals waiting for them, others had nurtured unattainable fantasies, but almost all got married and started families within a few years after liberation. And they worked hard—many with the U.S. Postal Service, which favored POWs and disabled veterans in hiring—always on the go, go, go, pulling extra shifts, holding two jobs, hammering birdhouses and whatnot in the garage for the neighbors. So much to do and no sense moping around.

Some have stayed put—they had seen enough of this godforsaken world. Others have traveled back to Europe to sift sand and shrapnel from landing beaches and walk the perimeters of stalags long dismantled and forgotten.

They emerged from captivity radically changed, of course, hardened into pack rats, food scroungers, insomniacs, claustrophobiacs, and frequently remote husbands and fathers in the grip of demons and nightmares. The wife of one POW recalls her man grinding his teeth in his sleep, mercilessly

RESTRICTED

HEADQUARTERS
EUROPEAN THEATER OF OPERATIONS
MIS-X Detachment
Military Intelligence Service
APO 887

SECURITY CERTIFICATE
for
Ex-Prisoners of War

1. Some activities of American Prisoners of War within German prison
camps must remain secret not only for the duration of the war against the
present enemies of the United States but in peace-time as well. The interests of American prisoners of war in Japanese camps require mainten-
ance of the strictest security on the activities of American prisoners
of war in German camps. The interests of American prisoners in the event
of future wars, moreover, demand that the secrets of this war be rigor-
ously safeguarded.

2. I therefore understand that under Army Regulations and the laws
of the United States, during my military service and later, as a civilian,
I may not reveal, discuss, publish or otherwise disclose to unauthorized
persons information on escape from enemy prison camps or evasion in enemy
occupied territory, clandestine organizations among prisoners of war, any
means of outwitting captors or of promoting intelligence activities within prison camps.

3. The authorship of articles or stories on these subjects is specifically forbidden and military personnel are warned that they will be
held strictly accountable for the communication of such information to
other persons who may subsequently publish or disclose such material.

4. I understand that any information suggested by the above mentioned categories is SECRET and must not be communicated to anyone other
than the agency designated by AC of S, G-2, War Department, or the corres-
ponding organization in overseas theaters of operations.

Name (Print) ....Signed......................

Rank..P.F.C..................ASN..................Dated.May 8, 1945....

Unit.17.J.D.,.4325 USAHP...............With.CARLETON J. SWEETSER
                    APO 887   2 d LT MAC
194-215

RESTRICTED

Some former POWs were coerced at war's end to sign this document from Military
Intelligence. Called a Security Certificate, it required a POW to keep silent about
his experiences for the supposed protection of prisoners still held in Japan and for
those of "future wars." According to Charles Walsh, a Veterans Affairs counselor,
failure to talk about their captivity has had devastating psychological effects for
many former POWS.

raking them together, and it took a "year of hugging" to soothe that away. Many former POWs drank too much. Some hit their wives. Others compensated for the cruelty they had seen by making kindness and generosity their guiding principles, maybe too much for their own good. More than a few developed intense empathy for victims of the Holocaust. All were scarred.

Now many former POWs are talking. Their stories, the gory and degrading ones that defined their lives, reveal their etched faces. At the same time, their faces animate their stories. These men realize that poison needs out. They have seized the opportunity to heal, and right behind the poison has appeared the light of their indomitable spirits.

In 2004 and 2005, Americans observed the 60th anniversaries of the turning points of WW II in Europe: D-Day, the Battle of the Bulge, the final defeat of the German Army, and the liberation of POW and concentration camps. The country was reminded that its WW II veterans were rapidly dying away, the attrition rate escalating with each passing year.

The mortality rate is even higher for former POWs, who suffer from more health problems than veterans as a whole. Four of the men featured here passed away in 2005 and 2006. Chesley Russell, at age 96, the oldest of the group, died just a few months after having his photograph taken. Emanuel "Rumpie" Rempelakis died at 84 from a stroke. A tough customer, he had flung himself three times from burning planes over Europe—the all-time bailout record, he suggested, none too humbly. Vit Krushas, who spoke wistfully of joining his deceased wife in a nearby cemetery, got his wish at 83. Emaciated from not eating, he seemed to be saying goodbye at the last ex-POW meeting he attended. And Don Simpson, five years after the death of his beloved Mary, the girl he loved since boyhood, died in 2006.

Old bones willing, on a weekly basis the former POWs featured in *Journey Out of Darkness* meet at VA offices in Boston and Brockton. Members of the Boston group gather first for morning coffee, and then after the official session many of them hang around for lunch; and so kibitzing and therapy merge across the day. Founded in 1981, the Boston support group is the oldest of its kind in the country. Active membership has fallen steeply, to less than 20 in 2006, as the men become incapacitated or pass away.

According to ex-POW Frank Molinari, most of the groups' early members are dead. "Rittenberg, Elwell, Carboy, Calabruzzo, Abruzzi," he says, "all alcoholics, all killed themselves." Simple cause and effect, he says. "The guys who are still alive are the ones who got the help," who allowed the comfort of peers to change their lives—no matter how much it hurt.

Cosmo Fabrizio, a member of the Brockton group, has watched many former POWs come into their circle over the years. The "green ones," he says, tense up when the conversation comes around to the war. Cosmo urges the men to "let it out." Some do, but others resist and stop attending.

Many former POWs not only resist counseling, but fail to collect POW disability payments. Some hold bitter grudges against the VA, which for decades required former POWs to prove that their medical conditions resulted from captivity. To this day, POWs from WW II face tougher disability standards than POWs from the Vietnam and Persian Gulf Wars. Other former POWs may simply be unaware of their options. Tony Dears of the Brockton group, captured during the Anzio landings, did not learn about POW disability payments or VA counseling until the mid-1990s. A guy paving his driveway filled Tony in.

Still other POWs, self-reliant products of the Depression, are just too proud to accept help. Bob Noble, an outspoken former POW, cannily advises men with this attitude to "do it for your spouse," so she will receive benefits after her man dies. An estimated one-third of former POWs from WW II are not receiving adequate care, despite stepped-up efforts over the last 25 years by the VA and organizations such as American ex-Prisoners of War.

Charles Walsh runs both the Boston and Brockton support groups. He served in the Army in Germany during the 1960s and freely states that he did not like it much. That admission lends Walsh credibility with the former POWs who were more than happy to return to civilian life—hence their willingness to sign objectionable documents, no matter the stench. Now, with a few exceptions, they muse pacifistically about war as a flawed means of resolving conflict. They do not want anyone else to go through what they endured.

"You couldn't have a war if the kids didn't show up," says Walsh. "Wouldn't that be great?"

His men, says Walsh, invariably suffer from post traumatic stress disorder —feelings regurgitate, he says, they bite you in the ass—in addition to chronic illnesses stemming from malnutrition, exposure to freezing temperatures, combat wounds, and beatings received in the camps. In many cases, the symptoms of PTSD have burst forth in old age as the men face the stress of retirement, declining health, and the death of friends and family members. Survival guilt is common, as is a sense of powerlessness. Walsh tells the former POWs to stop asking why, because there is no good answer to that question. Rather he exhorts them to celebrate their lives as a way of redeeming their buddies who "died in their places."

Meetings start with recitation of the Pledge of Allegiance and a moment of silence for "all those who didn't make it back." Sometimes Walsh adds a reference to the dead of the Iraq and Afghan wars. The men stand with uncommon rigor, hands over hearts, their voices ragged. They face a large American flag, side by side with a black POW/MIA flag. Walsh pins them to the wall for every meeting, even though the securing of objects to surfaces inside a federal building is strictly forbidden. "The flag means everything to them," he says. "So sue me."

Then the floor opens to comments and questions about VA disability issues, current events, whatever feelings or memories come up. Sometimes Walsh leads the men in relaxation techniques. They have taken field trips to WW II exhibitions and memorial events, but it is best not to gather former POWs in small rooms, he has discovered, or expect them to ride bunched up in elevators. Too much like the cattle cars, the stifling barracks.

"There's magic in the group," says Walsh. By listening to each others' war tales—"the high point and low point of their lives, at the same time"—a healing process occurs for some of the men that could not happen in one-on-one therapy sessions. The camaraderie opens reluctant minds and restores bitter hearts.

For all their neuroses, for all their pain, Walsh is continually impressed with the strength of character of his POWs. "They are not particularly religious, but they have a lot of faith. Each one of these guys is a historical figure ...I love them dearly."

Prisoner of war is a strange term—everyone in a war is its prisoner on some level, beholden to the decisions of governments and generals, to the whims of weather and ricocheting bullets. A soldier's head may rise up from cover and be blasted away this moment, but not the next. Every combat participant in the modern era suffers from a profound lack of freedom over one's survival. In the era of "strategic bombing" of civilians, every person in the path of war loses freedom; everyone becomes its prisoner.

The official POWs of WW II, however, were at the same time forced out of the war and further into it. They became prisoners *inside* the war, cargo moved and stored like tanks or grain or garbage, a small group among the millions of souls caught in the Reich's bloody maw. A POW's crime? Turning left when he should have turned right. Not being on the right side of a shifting line. Not dying—that can be a crime in wartime, not dying in a blaze of glory. The Japanese directed this attitude at both enemy POWs and their own captured soldiers: better they kill themselves than endure the shame and humiliation of surrender. Yanks and Brits gained some protection from the Geneva Convention, but the treaty was easily and frequently ignored (and never followed with Russian POWs, who were starved or worked to death by the hundreds of thousands).

Behind the Nazi wire, the POWs wondered. Are we winning the war? Will we be liberated by Christmas? In '44 and '45, as word of Allied victories leaked into camps, they asked new questions. Will Hitler hold us as bargaining chips? Is the rumor true, that they'll shoot us as revenge for Dresden and Berlin? Or just out of spite for losing? Wondering was all they had, for POWs were indeed men without. Without guns, without enough to eat, without a mission—they were reduced, ground-down men. In the long hours of boredom and suffering they asked themselves, Are we forgotten?

No, they are not—at least not to each other. Buoyed by the solace of their peers, the former POWs in this book have worked hard to heal themselves. But war trauma, especially the horror of combat followed by the humiliation of captivity, defies complete healing. To their immense credit, these men have contained the pain and stopped it from spreading. They have staked out decent, if troubled lives around the healed areas.

That in itself is a kind of victory, deeply drawn on the faces of old men.

CHAPTER 5

Our Bound Histories:
The Photographer's Quest

"For our generation, you don't show pride in your country," says Jorg Meyer, a native German. "You never raise the flag. To me, flags have no meaning."

Flags, however, have great meaning for the American POWs of Nazi Germany who Meyer has photographed. When he arrives at their homes, there is always a Stars and Stripes flying on a pole out front, waving from a porch railing, or pasted on the door in the apartment hallway. Sometimes the American flag is plastered on a window, colors facing out, at once a public declaration and a shade.

Meyer emigrated from Germany to the United States in 1995, at age 27, in the tracks of his girlfriend when she took a research fellowship at Harvard Medical School. It was his "big escape," says Jorg, away from a family that did not understand his dreams of taking great photographs—an escape, ultimately, away from being "seen the way people wanted to see me" and toward something larger and more promising. As a child he had received postcards of Indian cliff dwellings in Arizona from his traveling grandfather—the grandfather *in* his life, Jorg asserts, as opposed to the other one —a man who had survived World War II as a boy and gone to work translating for the occupying Americans. Jorg became fascinated with America and his grandfather's tales of a boundless, chaotic realm beyond the ocean. There, perhaps, he could photograph faces that reflected the wide-open spaces of a new land, faces with eyes unclouded by the oppressions of history.

Jorg Meyer

"Germans today still feel the guilt," Jorg states, about the actions of his countrymen during WW II. The guilt can be general, for the nation, and particular, for a family member. One of Jorg's grandfathers, his father's father, was an SS officer. This man, Georg Meyer, was captured by the Russians at the end of the war, and then managed to survive the Siberian gulag and return home in 1952. Some people considered him a victim for what he had endured. Georg Meyer avoided his sons for the most part, but for some unstated reason attended Jorg's christening in 1968. Days after, he committed suicide by shooting himself.

As a schoolboy, Jorg and fellow students were encouraged to confront the shame of the Nazi era; he recalls feeling traumatized by a trip to the Dachau concentration camp, an hour's drive from his hometown of Munsing. Over 200,000 people from 30 countries were enslaved and brutalized by the Nazis at Dachau. At least 30,000 died in the camp, some from barbaric medical experiments. Most were Jews, but enslaved too were communists, gypsies, clergy, Jehovah's Witnesses, homosexuals, social democrats, and every type of undesirable human conceivable to the Nazi mind. The word, Dachau, like Auschwitz, needs no explanation; it is a black and fixed fact in the German psyche.

Jorg had never met a Jew while growing up in Germany. In the United States, however, he has made Jewish friends and even attended a Jewish holiday celebration. Nonetheless, he says, at the event, "I felt incredibly guilty, and I hoped they wouldn't notice my German accent."

Many young Germans, Jorg asserts, have gone to Israel and worked in kibbutzim—penance performed by children for their grandparents' sake. We are different, the young Germans say in words and deeds. They work the field with Israelis. They speak softly. We are different than the other ones.

After high school, Jorg chose civil service duty instead of a stint in the German military. For two years he worked in a hospital as a nurse's aide, performing duties such as washing patients and bringing corpses down to the morgue. He grew to admire the courage displayed by many of the older, infirm patients who faced suffering and death without complaint. The words of one old man, though, are scarred in his mind.

"If Hitler were alive today," the man told him, "I'd put you against the wall and shoot you for not being in the military." Jorg—born on the Fuhrer's birthday, as are roughly 1/365th of all Germans—shot back: "Hitler would shoot a decrepit old man like you."

Jorg's father, Hans Meyer, is a Lebensborn child. Lebensborn, meaning "fountain" or "source of life," was a Nazi program designed to enrich German racial lines with Aryan blood. It involved a network of special facilities where "racially pure" women gave birth to children fathered by SS officers and other men of quality. The mothers and children received special care at Lebensborn homes. Reischfuhrer Heinrich Himmler, a staunch believer in eugenic theories dictating extermination of inferior races and propagation of superior ones, often visited the nurseries to gaze upon the cherubic faces of the next generation of Germen supermen.

Lebensborn children received baptism in a pseudo-Christian ceremony under a Nazi flag. The ritual was lit by *kerzenleuchters,* which are wall-mounted candelabras manufactured at that time by the slave laborers of Dachau.

"It's our duty to teach our kids the nature of evil," says Jorg, who has three young children—German and American citizens. "It's not about Germans in particular, it's mankind in general."

A few months after Jorg came to America, he happened upon a Veteran's Day parade in downtown Boston (Veteran's Day in Germany is downplayed and has no parades). He was intrigued by the rows of old men marching, adorned in fragments of old military uniforms and VFW hats. Some moved casually, while others held themselves parade-ground rigid, eyes front and seemingly oblivious to applause. These veterans struck Jorg as "visually interesting," a comment that glosses over the connection he began to feel toward the men. He wanted to photograph them, but did not yet feel accomplished enough in his art.

Eight years later in the spring of 2003, by then well established as a portrait photographer with a studio in Boston, Jorg read in *The Boston Globe* that American WW II veterans were rapidly dying, several every day. A sense of urgency came over him. Now is the time to do this, he decided. Now I am ready.

By calling around to area VA hospitals, Jorg learned about support groups for former POWs in Boston and Brockton. He met with the groups and his purpose came into focus. These men were more than soldiers who had rolled through his country, firing weapons and tossing chocolate bars to children. They forced him to consider his exile. Jorg had emigrated from Germany only to find American men who had suffered greatly in the world he had left behind. Some had even been held at Stalag VIIA in Moosburg, just 20 miles from Jorg's hometown. He had never known there was a camp there, and now all vestiges of Stalag VIIA are gone except for a fountain built by a former French prisoner.

Six decades after their liberation, these ex-POWs seemed to be prisoners of their experiences. Their stories were harrowing and they spoke of abandonment during and after the war, of misplaced shame and guilt. These men, Jorg felt, deserved more respect than they had received; they deserved not to feel ashamed for what had happened to them, for events beyond their control. They deserved the honor of undivided attention.

Each portrait photograph in this book is about one person in his environment, and nothing else. One old man, finally recognized. Captured, but freely. "It's important for them," says Jorg, important that they become everything within his camera frame.

A bit of a throwback, he works with 4-by-5 sheet film, similar to the kind that was used for the ex-POWs' service photographs, when they were young and hard-trained to fight wars. Jorg sets up his shots meticulously, cajoling the former POWs to turn this way and that. Photographer and subject chatter and joke, and as he takes Polaroid test shots he asks them about their wartime experiences—so they are at once here, now, and back there, then.

There is no push-and-click, nothing too modern; to expose film, Jorg turns a lever on the side of his camera.

In close-ups, Jorg watches for those moments when something vital emerges from the men's faces, when they reveal aspects of themselves that they may not have known, or remembered, still existed. And they in turn give back, allowing Jorg to confront his country's legacy, and his family's stain, with a measure of freedom that he could never have realized before.

"We have a shared history," says Jorg, "and I am touched by how they have lived on."

CHAPTER 6

The Art of Survival: Gabe Paiva's Story

A cousin on his mother's side got on his tail and would not let up. Finally, about nine years ago, he wrote it all down and God knows it was not a pleasant task, taking over a year to complete. "I had to comb my memories," he says, "pulling things out" that did not want out. Until then the details had stayed in the unspoken dark of his mind. "I felt that I shouldn't impose my story on anyone," states Gabriel Dias Paiva, Jr., American POW of the Imperial Government of Japan, 1942–1945.

The 58-page document that Gabe extracted from himself is stark and sad, uncompromising and relentlessly unsentimental. It begins the day of his first discharge from the Navy on July 23, 1940, after six years of peacetime service, and ends the day of his second and last discharge on April 12, 1946. He recorded his story for the family history, never thinking it would go much further. That it has, "I'll accept it," he says.

Gabe lives in a Department of Veterans Affairs nursing hospital, set in the woods of Bedford, Massachusetts, a commuter's suburb of Boston. The hospital's floors are waxed and clean and on this day the walls have been splashed with Christmas decorations, like a fourth-grade classroom. Men pass by sunken into wheelchairs, turning the wheels with stern expressions as they head to and from rehab, the dining hall, or the TV room. Gabe's quarters, which he shares with an empty bed, are small and Spartan. His room has no window; in fact, there are several walls between this room and a window. But no matter: he is an old submariner, having served inside the heavy metal casing of a 1930s-era "pig boat," and he does not require a horizon. After the war, Gabe lived alone in small rooms and studio

Gabe Paiva

apartments. Tight places have never bothered him, as long as they are quiet and comfortable.

Here he is secreted away. A little TV on a retractable arm hovers near his twin bed, and the sheet and blanket are tucked in, shipshape. Most of Gabe's books and papers and keepsakes are stashed on a shelf above his bureau. He is willing to loan out a copy of his wartime tale, if someone cares to ask, but he worries that it may not come back. In those pages burn the white-hot center of his life.

Of course, his life did not end there; the embers have burned long and low. Gabe returned from overseas, late 1945, in bad shape. At Chelsea Naval Hospital, perched on a bluff overlooking Boston Harbor, he received treatment for amoebic dysentery, parasitic worms, and the chronic effects of long-term malnutrition. There they told him that his father had suffered a stroke back in '43, upon learning that his Gabriel had been taken by the Japanese. The old man, a former landlord and maker of Portuguese sausage, could no longer walk or speak or wash himself.

When Gabe emerged from the hospital he took it easy for a year. "My fun," he says, "was just sitting down and knowing I was secure." Family members thought it peculiar that he did not live it up like other vets. They could not begin to fathom "the fatigue that had penetrated my being."

He might have explained his weariness, ugly truth and all, if someone had pressed him. But former POWs were not encouraged to volunteer information. "They didn't want us to say much," says Gabe. "To write about it or talk about it, we had to get permission. Everyone just kept quiet, not just myself."

Besides, he says, when you have been a POW, "people judge."

Believe it or not, Gabe considered reenlisting in the Navy. He seesawed back and forth, but finally decided against it because he did not want to go through another war. So he tried his hand at house painting, grinding lenses for an optician, and then clerking at the post office. In each job his legs throbbed and swelled from standing, thanks to beri beri and pellagra and God-knows-what tropical diseases. Gabe became a civilian employee of the Navy in 1948, working as a security guard/fire fighter at the Watertown Arsenal. The nightly patrols kept the circulation going, the swelling at bay. His father died the next year—a casualty, it could be said, of the son's war.

Year after year Gabe worked at the Arsenal as it churned out guns and tanks for the Korean and Vietnam Wars, and by night he relaxed, read history, and made dinner on his small gas stove in his rented room. He kept to a strict regimen of jogging and swimming at a local gym. The old stamina, though, would never return. No matter how much he rested, no matter how well he cared for his battered body, there was no making up for what had been lost.

"I felt exhausted all the time," he says. "I was dragged out, pooped." He adds: "But I don't cry about it."

Gabe retired in 1966. He never married or had children because he just did not have the energy for it. Simple as that, he says. The tiredness was so deep. The weight of what he had experienced, so heavy. The pleasure of just sitting in a soft chair, so well earned. His need to preserve internal equilibrium became absolutely imperative. After all, Gabe returned from what he calls hell, where four out of ten Allied POWs did not survive captivity. In retirement he rested and read and exercised, and he watched the raucous world and startled awake from nightmares that have never ceased. In 2004 he injured his hip and had no choice but to move into the VA hospital.

Now he sits in the new visiting room—a sterile, untrammeled space—his wheelchair parked next to the couch. Gabe announces that he could live another ten years, and why not? He might pass the hundred mark, you never know. The art of survival that he mastered in the POW camps is quite useful, actually, in old age. "Let's say you're an old man," he says, coyly. "If you decide one day to go to bed and not wake up, you're not going to wake up." Vice-versa, you want to wake up, you probably will. Put away all negative feelings, he explains, or they will destroy you.

Later the fluorescent lights in the room go out, as if twilight has suddenly fallen. Gabe has it figured right away. The motion sensors detected nothing alive in the room, so why bother. He kicks his old legs, like a pony, and the lights snap back on. "No one moved," he says. "You have to keep moving."

What makes a man, treated for years with incomparable cruelty, keep moving? Where did he find the ability to put the negative feelings, the hatred away? How can Gabe Paiva say, "Love, hope, and charity, that's what counts," after what he has seen of hate, despair, and savagery?

After Thanksgiving, the mood and pace changed. Crews at the Cavite Naval Yard in the Philippines worked around the clock building bomb shelters, reinforcing walls, and moving ammo and mines out to Sunset Beach, 12 miles away. It was, Gabe says, as if they knew the storm was coming. The breakneck work continued right through the Japanese attack on Pearl Harbor on December 7, 1941. Two days later, Gabe missed breakfast when Japanese observation planes sent air-raid alarms wailing, and the next day the first bombs fell in a three-hour raid that destroyed much of the Navy yard and killed 800 sailors, Marines, and Filipino workers.

At his station inside the mine and ammunition depot, Gabe did not belong. He was a fish out of water, Torpedo Man First Class (specialty: mine warfare) on temporary duty waiting for a good sub to surface. Sitting on a powder keg had not been the idea when he reenlisted in 1940, just five days after his discharge. "I had wanted to try the outside," says Gabe of his civilian interlude, during which he returned home to his Portuguese corner of Cambridge, Massachusetts, flat broke, no job on the horizon, and let us just say his stepmother did not greet him like the prodigal son. Like a slap across the face, Gabe realized he was Navy through and through—even though he could see the war coming.

Not one bomb hit the ammunition depot. But something detonated within Gabe, spreading a strong fear that "would leave its mark on my psyche," he writes in his chronicle. "It is fear for one's life that causes a man to keep ducking and avoiding bullets and bombs, yes moving fast to stay alive."

The aerial assault continued for weeks, and in place of a flock of pigeons that had fled the depot entrance appeared one white dove. "It seemed perfectly calm and peaceful and was there in the same spot day and night," writes Gabe. "Catholics, Protestants, and Jews marveled, taking it as a sign of Divine Protection." At the same time, he was shocked to see drunken Marines patrolling the streets of Cavite City, "wristwatches up to their elbows."

On Christmas Day, U.S. forces drenched the depot in gun powder and blew it to high heaven, then sailed to Mariveles on Manila Bay across from the island fortress known as Corregidor. First thing, Gabe ran to the radio tunnel and hiked his life insurance, made out to his father, from $1,000 to $10,000. Mariveles was an ominous place. Wild hogs ran through the bush at night, letting out loose, strangled screams. Japanese bombers spun down out of the blinding, midday sun, as if born from it.

For the next four and a half months, they held on to Corregidor. Food was scarce and the shelling and bombing relentless. When Japanese troops

Gabe Paiva, Navy submariner, visits New York City in the spring of 1939 for the opening of the World's Fair.

advanced on land, Gabe became a runner during fire fights. It was his job to scout the enemy and carry messages between units. As he ran from tree to tree, as he dove behind rocks with bullets ripping by just inches away, he wore on his finger a talisman for the tightest spots—his mother's wedding ring.

Gabe had received the ring after Susanna Paiva died of influenza in 1918, one of twenty-one million people killed by the pandemic. The disease was brought into Boston by soldiers returning from World War I. Gabe remembers standing next to his ma's deathbed, just four years old, a little sack hung around his neck filled with camphor to ward off the germs. Now on Corregidor the ring made him feel as if she ran beside him, waving the bullets away.

A submarine, the USS *Trout,* docked at Corregidor in February 1942 and took on 20 tons of gold and silver from banks in Manila. Gabe learned that the skipper was Captain Frank Wesley Fenno, his old commander on the USS-45 in Panama. "I was so very much tempted," he writes, "to travel the four miles, the length of the island, to see if they would take me aboard." Instead he stayed and the smart money left for Pearl Harbor. Gabe grew skinny and frazzled and by spring Japanese shelling had enshrouded the island in a cloud of dust.

Finally on May 5, 1942, General Wainwright surrendered American forces on Corregidor. Aware of harsh Japanese treatment of prisoners, Gabe nonetheless felt relieved to have survived. Following orders, he destroyed his gun, knives, and even the "precious hair clippers that would be sorely missed later."

Cabuatuan #3, north of Manila, was his first POW camp. Here tropical blisters broke out around Gabe's waist and crotch. His legs swelled up and his scrotum grew like a balloon due to malnutrition and vitamin deficiencies. A friend poked it with a stick, joking "Berri berri." Next he came down with dysentery, then constipation, then painful internal hemorrhoids. "I think they would have liked to have killed us all," Gabe says of his captors. He prayed constantly, using rosary beads he kept in a small bag. When the guards found the beads during searches, Gabe pointed at himself saying, "Christian, Christian," and they nodded and let him keep them.

The Japanese did not persecute the POWs for their religion. No, says Gabe, POWs were worthless and deserving of cruel treatment for allowing themselves to be captured, for not seeking out death as a Japanese soldier would have done. The POWs' lives had lost any intrinsic value. Gabe writes about three men caught escaping:

They were picked up walking toward town. Their explanation was that they were hungry and were seeking food. The three were taken back to camp and tied to stakes, beaten up, and left in the hot sun without food or water for 3 days. The whole camp was turned out to

This snapshot was taken at a photo studio in Japan, in September 1945, about three weeks after the end of the Pacific War. Gabe Paiva, seated, had gained 25 pounds since the liberation of the carbide factory where he was used as slave labor. Behind him are Australian ex-POWs A.E. Simpson and Alf Webb.

witness the execution. Three shallow graves had been dug about a foot and a half deep. They were stood at the edge. The firing squad fired, the bodies fell into the graves, and the Jap soldiers stepped forward firing their Lugar pistols into the bodies.

Gabe disguised his mother's wedding ring at Cabuatuan #3 by wrapping thread around it. However, one day during a work detail, a guard "sneaked up on top of me," says Gabe, "and saw my open palm." The thread had slipped, the gold shined through. It was too late. The guard wanted the ring. He demanded it. He pushed ten pesos, Japanese occupation money, at the prisoner. Knowing that he would be beaten if he did not surrender it—and then it would be taken nonetheless—Gabe handed his mother's wedding ring to the guard.

But he refused the payment. "I didn't want to have the sense that I sold it," he says.

Gabe made a second decision right there, for his own preservation, a decision that he would carry forward for the next three years and well beyond. "I didn't let it bother me. I couldn't afford to let it. Emotions can kill, negative emotions can damage the body." The loss of the ring steeled him, deadened him to endure. Only after liberation did he allow regret to seep back in. "I should have sewed it into my clothes," says Gabe, in his old age. "I should have done it another way."

In October 1942 Gabe and thousands of other POWs were put on board the *Nagata Maru*, a merchant ship built, according to a plate on deck, in Trenton, New Jersey, USA. The ship's three holds were crammed with 1,500 POWs, fed once a day. The *Nagata Maru* joined a convoy, hunted by American submarines, on a zigzagging course from Formosa to Japan. When a sub was sited, alarms sounded and the POWs were locked in their holds. The men, writes Gabe, "remained calm knowing there was nothing they could do to avoid whatever fate might have in store for them." Seven POWs died during the three-week ordeal, each given "a formal burial, wrapped and sewed in canvas and slipped over the side with Christian prayers."

The boat docked at Moji, Japan, around Thanksgiving Day. It had been nearly one year since Gabe had noticed preparations for a Japanese attack at Cavite Naval Base. He was sent to Tanagawa, one of the Osaka camps, where POWs were put to work moving earth and rocks for a submarine dry dock. They were sick and starving men, infested with cooties and lice from the sea voyage. Gabe asserts that he received no medical care from the Japanese during his years of captivity, except once for worms, but there was a building at Tanagawa set aside for men too ill to work. The POWs called it the morgue because only one man who entered there ever returned.

Breakfast was a bowl of watery rice porridge. Lunch, two small flour buns and two small balls of cooked rice. Supper, a bowl of rice with a side dish of daikon or misu broth. Just enough calories, Gabe says, to keep you on thin ice. In the evenings the men huddled around a few charcoal pits in the barracks. It was so cold his hands split open and many nights he could not fall asleep until three o'clock a.m. The POWs were awoken at five o'clock a.m. to begin work—ten days on, one day off. That winter, one third of the camp died.

In May 1943, as Allied forces began to recapture the Aleutian Islands, thousands of miles northeast of Japan, and U.S. Marines bled on the beaches of the Solomon Islands even further away to the south, Gabe was transported to the Umeda Bunsho POW Camp in Osaka. There Allied POWs became slave laborers for Nippon Tsuun, a company now known as Nippon Express, one of the world's largest shipping conglomerates. The men worked long days loading and unloading freight trains, barges, and boats. They carried toxic cargo up and down planks, shouldering poles with loads on each end. Gabe totally focused himself on survival. There was no room for prayer, no place for admitting the weakness that prayer depends upon. His writing about this period takes on a skewed, detached point of view:

> I have seen myself work chemicals in straw bags weighing 30 kilos with a total of 60 kilos on a pole walking out of a boat up inclined planks to the docks all day. That was a total of 130 pounds. When we first started to carry we suffered until we became hardened to heavy weight. We were worked by civilians and banged around when we displeased them with our work or otherwise.

"My body," he says now, "was crying all the time."

Gabe carried rice in 110-pound bags, heavier than his own depleted body. Sometimes when the guards turned away he dropped pig iron into the canal, to create loss, to feel in some minor way a part of the war effort. Once a cart full of pig iron fell on him and broke a couple of ribs. He contracted dengue fever (good for three days off duty) and scab-like lesions grew inside his lungs. The POWs' lower bodies bloated with fluid, from grueling work and malnutrition, and in the mornings they woke with swollen, puffed-up faces. The Japanese guards found this hilarious—look, look how well our American friends are fed! Civilians jeered as the men walked back and forth to the docks and freight yard, scraps of straw bound to their feet, ragged clothes matted to their bodies. "Horios," the people called out, dishonorable ones.

At night the POWs doubled up for warmth. A Marine who slept next to Gabe thanked him for information he had delivered as a runner in the Philippines—it had saved his life. Soon after, the man died in his sleep. That was the second time it had happened, Gabe waking up beside a dead body. "Not very pleasant," he writes, "when one is struggling under the same circumstances."

One poor fellow named John Welter, he remembers, weighed about 85 pounds on a tall frame. He seemed to have lost his spirit, and the low point came when a civilian truck driver cut Welter's head open with a shovel for stealing food. The next day, Gabe decided to start a fight with the truck driver. The two men struggled and Gabe, the vermin horio, fell backwards on a heap of coal. He writes: "The Jap came up with raised shovel ready to let me have it. I yelled at him to get off me. Welter dove at him with a football-style tackle." Taking the blame, Gabe got a slug in the mouth from a guard they called Punchy. But it was worth it. From that day forward, Welter recovered his dignity and his will to survive.

There was, it turned out, a right and a wrong way to receive a beating. The wrong way was to stand rigid and take it, like a man. The right way, the technique that minimized physical damage, was to roll away from the blows with arms up to deflect contact. But it did not always work—once a guard christened Rabbit Tooth struck Gabe so hard that his eardrum shattered. He let it heal on its own, despite the overwhelming pain, because he feared that the camp doctor (a POW) would infect it with an unsterilized instrument. That was a smart thing to do, he believes, letting the pain alone.

There was a right way, too, for a starving man to eat rice, not greedily but very slowly, holding it in the mouth for a long time. That way, states Gabe, the rice would break down chemically and allow the body to more easily absorb it. You had to be smart; you never turned down an opportunity to eat. He recalls devouring fried, crunchy silkworms discovered on the floor of a freight car. Delicious, like nothing else in the world. The POWs who did not starve, he says, stayed alive by a thread.

To be kept in that condition for 2 or 3 months would be torture, to live through more than 3 years was hell. Time stood still and seemed eternal. I lived another full lifetime. Toward the end as a prisoner, I would experience my nervous system breaking down. On occasion I would feel as though [I was] receiving a violent electric shock. I would stop in my work of carrying and fight this condition by the sheer force of will. When the war finally did end, I had felt instinctively that I could not have survived another winter.

American bombing of Japan, of industrial facilities and residential neighborhoods, escalated in 1945, and bombs fell less than a block from their POW camp at Umeda Station. In May, Gabe was among 60 men moved inland to Take Fu, a mountain town where he was forced to work in a factory. For months the POWs stood close to dangerous arc furnaces, without protective clothing, pushing together limestone and coke to make carbide, an alternative engine fuel. Many POWs had no shoes and resorted to wearing discarded shoe covers. Their ration of rice was further reduced and Gabe's weight fell below 100 pounds.

One day, the commander at the factory assembled the POWs and announced that they would get more to eat only when the Americans stopped bombing Japanese women and children—then and no sooner. Rumors circulated around the furnaces about orders to exterminate all POWs if the Japanese home islands were invaded. (These orders, in fact, did exist but were generally disregarded.)

After the war, Gabe poses with (left to right) his sister Mary, sister-in-law Dominica, and her sister Yolanda.

On August 14, 1945, word arrived that the war had ended. "No one can even imagine the relief and joy we felt," writes Gabe. But no tanks, no U.S. troops burst through the factory gates. The end of his suffering came gradually, his liberation doled out piece by piece. Armed Japanese guards remained on the premises for 19 days until the surrender terms were finalized. In the meantime, in the limbo between captivity and freedom, pallets of food and clothing floated into the mountain camp from the bellies of American bombers. (Some of the drops were poorly aimed, severely injuring POWs; Gabe "cursed the Americans for their recklessness.") The men stopped working and commenced eating day and night. Gabe gained back 25 pounds in just three weeks. His body soaked it up—it was, he says, the most remarkable thing, as if he were a sponge that had gone dry.

With a couple of Australian POWs, he took a day trip into the town of Take Fu. They happened upon a Japanese man, a tailor they had encountered at the carbide factory. The tailor sat cross-legged in the window of his shop, sewing a suit. He invited the soldiers into his home.

As there were no furniture or chairs, we sat on the straw mat that covered the floor. Speaking in Japanese he told us of a bomb being dropped and 60,000 people being killed...we met his wife and family and were received as friends. We returned another day bringing food as a gift...the tailor was so thankful that he gave each of us some of his possessions. I received a kimono and some China which I later gave away aboard ship in Yokahama Bay to souvenir hungry sailors.

It was mid-September by the time Gabe took a train to Yokahama—a city leveled by conventional bombing—and underwent delousing with DDT pesticide. Then he got aboard ship in the harbor. "I was so elated that this long ordeal was over that I had lost a sense of time," he writes. He filled out Navy paperwork, naming Rabbit Tooth for the sucker punch that broke his eardrum, and then traveled by air and sea in a blur of planes and boats, from bloody Iwo Jima to San Diego. On the train ride east from California he stared for long hours out the window, watching the towns and fields and stations rush by, surrounded on all sides by military personnel on their own journeys of dispatch and return, and finally Gabe arrived at Boston's South Station. It was there, in 1941 as he shipped out for the Philippines, that his father had warned him, son, not everyone who goes to war comes back the same way. Then he checked himself into Chelsea Naval Hospital, on the bluff above the harbor, and they told him about his father's stroke.

Now began the second stage of Gabe's survival, the era of holding together fractured mind and body, of recovery and resignation. Gabe waited in vain for the old energy to return. He worked his jobs—"I didn't live off Uncle Sam," he states emphatically—and he exercised with precision, a set number of minutes jogging and swimming per day, a set number of days per week. Nightmares about the camps persisted, so sleep held little rest

"The unconscious mind will do a job on you," Gabe knows, but what he could control, he did, searching for that neutral space beyond bitterness where emotions had no rule. He accessed his strengths and accepted his limits. He never let himself hate the Japanese or waste energy craving apologies from the Nippon Corporation. "They did what they had to do," he says. "That's war." Gabe Paiva summoned all that he had learned of survival to the steady task of making it through this day and the next.

It helped in the mid-1980s to join a VA support group for POWs. The other men had been imprisoned in Germany, some for only a few months, but "each one of them has suffered," says Gabe. "We experienced the same feelings." The same guilt, for having been captured, the same awful dread of living "in the hands of people who wanted you dead." The same anxiety when they returned home, the same nightmares taking them back against their wills.

What makes a man, treated for years with incomparable cruelty, keep moving? Where did he find the ability to put the negative feelings, the hatred away? How can Gabe Paiva say, "Love, hope, and charity, that's what counts," after what he has seen of hate, despair, and savagery?

The answer comes from the wedding ring and the hard things its loss made him do. It springs from the gentleness of his spirit, maintained in his

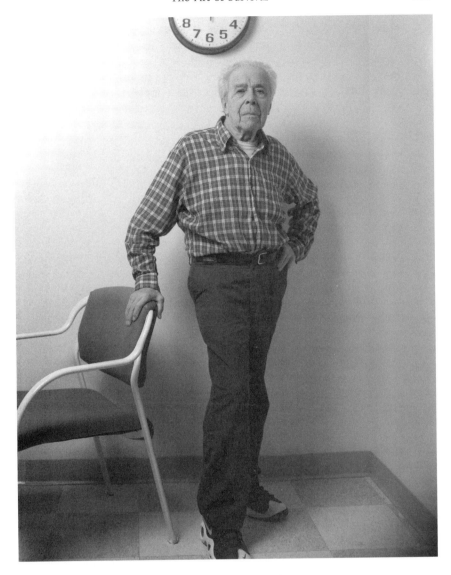

Gabe Paiva

self-exile from the noise and chaos of life. The answer, also, may be seeded in his first awakenings.

He remembers standing at his mother's death bed, four years on this earth, the pungent sack of camphor around his neck. But before that day he remembers playing in the yard and his ma coming to the window and calling for him to come inside. And the fava beans, he remembers how she would roast them Portuguese style until they were cooked but still hard. Gabe remembers Susanna putting one of these beans in her mouth and gently chewing. And then she took the bean from her mouth and fed it, soft and moist and infinitely sustaining, to Gabriel her youngest son.

CHAPTER 7

Tests of Faith: Where Is God?

JUDEN: SAM PALTER'S STORY

The story comes out in bursts, like flash lightning:

> All hell broke loose, mortar shells dropping everywhere, I threw my
> hand grenades, God knows if I pulled the pins, the platoon leader, he
> was green and ignored the sergeant who fought in North Africa, the
> screaming meemies going overhead, and just like that we're overrun,
> we had no chance, and there's a German standing over me with a rifle.

Right then, says Sam Palter, "I thought of my mother." The day was
August 7, 1944, Mortain, France, and he was 22 years old and two weeks
on the line, a replacement GI for the men broken and swept away in the
months after D-Day. Five combat-hardened panzer divisions had launched
a counter-offensive designed to drive the Allies back to the English Channel.
While Sam had fired at German positions before, he had never seen the
enemy until then. It was the worst day of his life, he says, the day he finally
saw the enemy.

Even though he had heard stories of how Germans treated Jews, what
happened next shocked him. Sam and seven other captured Americans were
trucked east. They stopped in a wooded area and got out. One of the soldiers guarding them asked if anyone spoke German. Sam stepped forward.
Then the soldier pointed at a short guy named Joe, slumped down against
a tree.

Sam Palter

"Jude? Jude?" asked the soldier. For a second, Sam wondered who he meant. Again the soldier pointed at Joe, with his dark hair and prominent nose. "Jude," he said, not a question anymore.

Sam shook his head, "Nein, nein," and explained that Joe was a Catholic, not a Jew. At least he thought he was Catholic, but certainly not Jewish. Or was he? Sam did not really know him, did not even know his last name. Something Italian. The soldier raised his rifle and leveled it at Joe. "Jude!" the German yelled, as if personally insulted.

Joe sat there, frozen. Did he understand what was happening? Sam strained back for German words, plucked them out of the chalky air of his high school classroom in Dorchester, Massachusetts. Not a Jew, he explained, absolutely not. Trust me, this man believes in Jesus who died for our sins. Nein, Jude, nein!

Moments passed…and the soldier lowered his rifle and turned away. It was over. Sam, now 83 years old, a retired postal worker and father of four, often wonders what would have happened if he had not spoken up. Would the guard have done it? Or was it some bizarre joke? The hatred had seemed real.

He tells this next part with razor-sharp precision. Before getting back in the truck, Sam spied a tree with a knothole. He moved over there slowly, casually, and leaned against the trunk. He made sure no one was watching. Then he grabbed the chain around his neck and pulled free his dog tags, two metal rectangles stamped with his name, rank, serial number, and a capital H for his religious designation. H for Hebrew. Sam stashed the dog tags in the knothole. He moved away from the tree, two ounces lighter.

That's how it happened. Who knows, his dog tags might still be there. Perhaps the tree sealed them over in the long years that have passed, grasped the metal to its wooden heart. Maybe some French kid, old now like Sam, found and kept them as a souvenir. Kids are always poking around trees. But Sam figures the tree was blown up or cut down or just died.

That night, he stayed in a barn next to pigs. ("That's not kosher, is it?" Sam jokes, sitting at his dining room table, a 1943 photo of himself in dress uniform on the wall over his shoulder.) Soon he found himself in a stinking boxcar with scores of other POWs—just like one of the Holocaust trains, he says—and five days later they arrived at a transit camp near Stalag VIIA. There Sam was given forms to fill out that would be sent to the International Red Cross. The basics: name, rank, serial number and, once again, religious affiliation.

Sam hesitated. He could put C, for Catholic. Or P, for Protestant. Or leave it blank, it was nobody's business. Or H, he could put H for Hebrew. Sam talked to an American paratrooper, an officer, and the man advised him to tell the truth. You are going to a good camp, the officer said, and besides it is just for the Red Cross. Sam was not sure; he thought of the soldier pointing his gun at Joe, yelling "Jude!" He thought of his dog tags buried in the tree, the H missing from his neck.

Sam is not sure why he wrote H for Hebrew on the form. Stubbornness, maybe. Or pride—his parents had escaped the pogroms in Russia, fled from Cossacks on horseback terrorizing the Jewish ghettoes in Odessa. His father, AWOL from the Russian Army, was sprung from jail by his little

Sam Palter has kept his POW dog tags, issued to every prisoner. When a POW died in captivity, the procedure was to break off one tag and send it to the Red Cross.

brothers and then all three stowed away on a boat to America. Yes, his mother and father were Russians by birth, then sloughed that off and became Americans, but they were always Jewish. Growing up, Sam rooted like crazy for Jewish baseball players, for Moe Berg, Harry Danning, and slugging Hank Greenberg. He lived in a Jewish neighborhood and learned Yiddish from his mother. No denying it, Sam Palter was nothing if not a Jew.

But he has to admit, maybe it was not pride. It could have been he was just naïve. Or maybe dazed from the terrible journey in the boxcar. He is not sure. Or this is possible, that he put an H on the form because the officer said so. That is what you did in the Army, obey officers. Another thing about armies, German or American: paperwork is redundant. Paperwork is endless. The original form went to the Red Cross and the carbon copy stayed with the Germans, slid into some file among millions of files. He should have known that about paperwork, says Sam.

Within a week he was moved to Stalag VIIA at Moosburg, an enormous camp that swelled to 100,000 POWs by war's end. Sam and fellow prisoners worked at the railroad yards in nearby Munich. Every day they repaired rails knocked out by Allied bombing. Other work crews arrived in boxcars: skeletal men in striped shirts with Stars of David stitched on their arms and "Juden" marked across their backs. Men from Dachau.

"That's when I knew that something bad was going on," says Sam. The Juden were treated much worse than the POWs, pushed around and kicked. Sam watched, helpless to intervene and overwhelmed with guilt. "What could I do? Nothing. And you had to look out for yourself, too." But it was not just guilt; he felt fortunate for not having a Star of David on his arm, for not getting beaten.

The POWs worked at the railroad yards through the fall and into the winter—unpaid slave labor. Sam appears uncomfortable calling it that, but his wife will not mince words; it was slave labor. Barbara and Sam banter and tease liberally, the prerogative of 57 years of marriage. When he claims that the pain and numbness in his legs started only a few years ago, she scoffs, "You've always walked funny." Ever since the war, she says. He rolls his eyes. His hip hurts, he admits, from that day the POWs refused to work on the tracks unless they were fed better. Sam translated the demands to a guard. The guard's counter offer: a rifle butt into Sam's hip.

It was a record-cold winter in 1945. Sam wrapped toilet paper around his feet and slept shivering in a barracks with a stove fueled only by bunk slats. If you burned too many slats, you would crash through on top of the poor guy underneath. Then one Sunday morning, as he shaved, a guard stormed into the barracks and started shouting names. "Silverstein," he yelled. "Greenberg, Palter." Jewish names spit from the German's mouth. A backlog of paperwork, evidently, had been properly reviewed. Numbers had been connected with names. Names had been sifted, categorized, underlined. The word, Hebrew, found.

"I thought I was rid of it," says Sam. "I thought it was over."

The Germans moved all identifiable Jewish POWs—regardless of nationality, for Juden trumped everything else—to a separate barracks. A ghetto, a *schetl*. They slept on a concrete floor. Their rations were cut to starvation levels. Although he was not a very religious man, Sam prayed every day. Then one month after their segregation, the Jewish POWs were sent back to their original barracks.

Why, Sam does not know. Why they were not sent to a concentration camp, the fate of Jewish POWs at other camps, that is a mystery, too. Sam knows an American POW, Philip Dantowitz, who was pegged for being Jewish and sent to the notorious Berga concentration camp, a satellite of

Sam Palter as a young soldier.

Buchenwald. At Berga, 20 percent of the GIs died from starvation, beatings, or overwork.

In late February Sam was among hundreds of POWs, Jews and Gentiles alike, shifted to Stalag 18C in Austria, at the foothills of the Alps. The place made a hell of a first impression: three men hung dead from a rafter outside the camp. The conditions were filthy and degrading, and Sam lost 40 pounds over the next two and a half months. There was nothing redeeming at 18C, nothing but misery as the wasting-away men worked at a nearby potato farm, received no mail or Red Cross parcels, and passed rumors, originating from the guards, that Hitler had ordered the execution of all POWs if Germany lost the war. Typhus decimated the Russian compound. Nothing redeeming, Sam remembers, except Passover.

It was late April, new spring. The son of a rabbi conducted the Passover readings, the *Haggedah*, about the exile and slavery of the Jews in Egypt, followed by their exodus to the Promised Land. These Jews of 18C, of course, had no means to make unleavened bread. They had no salt to sprinkle, to represent the dried-up tears of persecution, and they had no bitter herbs to recall the bitterness of captivity. Certainly, there was no *seder* feast to celebrate deliverance. They kept their voices low. Lookouts stood at the door watching for Nazis. But still they held Passover and the evil of their world did, finally, pass.

On May 9, 1945, two days after Germany's unconditional surrender, the Third Division of the U.S. Army discovered Stalag 18C. It was the last POW camp liberated in Europe, the "forgotten prison camp." Jack Bell, a reporter riding with the Third, filed a story that appeared in *The Boston Daily Globe*. The headline declared, *Bay State Soldiers Freed from Nazi Prison*. Bell watched the POWs rush out the gate and wrote, "A river flows past and thousands are bathing in the sunlight though the water is icy from nearby Alpine snows. The whole camp is tense because the war is over and every man is crying, 'Get us out of this godawful hole.'" Many of the POWs weeped as they gave Bell their names to be sent home to loved ones.

Service photos of Private Samuel Palter (the same photo on his dining room wall) and four other POWs—taken before they left home, before they learned of the world—accompanied the story. Below these sharp, young men in their dress uniforms ran an article about proposed war crimes trials for captured Nazis Rudolph Hess and Hermann Goering, and below that ran another story headlined *Kin Overjoyed by Globe's News of Prisoners*.

"When I got home, I tried to block it all out," says Sam, who seldom spoke about his war experiences, not even to his wife. On the first night of their honeymoon, he startled awake from a nightmare. Barbara wanted to know what he had dreamed, wanted to ask him what was wrong, but she decided to let it go. He would talk when he was ready. He did not talk very much, it turned out, until he retired from the Postal Service and sought counseling almost 40 years later.

About that time, 1986, Sam got in a spat with a wisecracking columnist for *The Boston Herald* named Howie Carr. In the middle of a piece mocking the Registry of Motor Vehicles for issuing red-white-and-blue license plates, Carr sneered, "This is the dumbest thing to come out of the Registry since the 'EX-POW' plates. Why don't we have an 'EX-CON' series?" Now Sam had run into a lot of loudmouth idiots in his day who equated POWs with criminals and cowards, but this was too much, out there for everyone to read. He blew his top, called the *Herald,* and hollered at Carr but good. "Did you serve?" Sam asked him repeatedly, but received no answer.

The newspaper printed his letter to the editor. "Obviously, Carr knows nothing about ex-POWs, nor is he very much interested," Sam wrote, concluding the letter in dignified, restrained fashion: "I would hope that our

Sam Palter

individual and combined time spent in enemy prison camps was not in vain, as was indicted by Carr's attitude." It helped, a lot, getting that off his chest.

Sam has not stopped expressing himself since and now it is not so painful for him to remember, not so bad to hash it all over and still not have the answers. The story is enough in itself. Nein, Jude, nein! The dog tags stowed in the tree. The H he wrote on the form. The striped men at the railroad yards, with the Stars of David on their arms. Passover at 18C. The meaning of being a Jew.

HOLY GHOST SOUP: ANTHONY DEARS'S STORY

It was his first night back in the States, after nearly three years away, and Anthony Dears could not wait one minute longer.

The Army had shipped him around enough, already. From Boston to basic training in Arkansas to some place in North Africa—they kept you moving so fast you didn't know where you were—then the Anzio beachhead in Italy where Anthony fought his way inland for nine days. At this point in the general carnage of things he was wounded and held prisoner

Anthony Dears

in Germany, but he emerged 16 months later, thinner than a rail, and it was go here, go there, all over again: France, England, back across the ocean to Boston, then straightaway to Camp Miles Standish just a few miles from his home in Brockton, Massachusetts. You can call your folks in the morning, soldier, they told him.

"I jumped the fence," says Anthony.

At eleven o'clock he knocked on the door of the house where he had lived since arriving as a boy from Portugal in 1933. He knocked on the door of the house where he would live for the next 60 years of his life, to this very day. His mother appeared in the doorway. She had been sleeping; she saw him and screamed; she grabbed her Antonio and would not let go. His father was there too, happy beyond words to see his son, and shocked to look at him, too. Anthony had withered from 175 to 119 pounds.

Right away, Mary Dears heated up a bowl of Holy Ghost soup. "I used to love it," says Anthony, "and I still do." A staple of Catholic feast celebrations, Holy Ghost soup is an earthy, long-simmering brew made from meat, bone marrow, chicken, cabbage, onion, and garlic, fragranced with bay and mint leaves, and poured on top of thick Portuguese bread. That night he jumped the fence, the soup that poured from his ma's ladle into Anthony's greedy body tasted very, very good.

He went back to Camp Standish in the morning and turned himself in. Miraculously, the duty officer let him off the hook. Anthony was honorably discharged within a few months and his mother kept making him Holy Ghost soup until she died at the age of 100.

Anthony is only 81. On this weekend in July, he plans on attending the Feast of the Blessed Sacrament in New Bedford, billed as the largest Portuguese feast in the world. He will try the Holy Ghost soup there and bring along Andrew, the son of the young couple who live, rent free, in part of his house. Andrew, a first grader, likes the carousels at the feasts, likes diving into cages full of colorful plastic balls. Squirming around, says Anthony, as if he is swimming. The old POW goes to as many feasts as possible, throughout the region, and he is always on the lookout for a free bowl of the Holy Ghost. That is a good excuse by itself to get in the car.

All of which makes perfect sense, because Anthony Dears is a very devout man who prays daily and gives to the church. He also says that he does not believe in God.

Anthony's faith, woven of bedtime prayers and Sunday services, unraveled at three stalags: 344 in Lamsdorf, Poland; IIIB in Furstenburg, Germany; and IIB in nearby Hammerstein. The last straw had to be the bitter-cold, forced march away from converging Russian and American troops in the final months of the war. The Nazis marched Anthony and droves of Allied POWs in huge circles around Germany and Central Europe, his column passing through the same town at least three times during several weeks. The men trudged and trudged and many collapsed from malnutrition and dysentery. As artillery rounds fell on all sides, questions besieged Anthony.

"Why is He letting this happen?" he asked. "How is this possible if there is a god?" Those questions intersected the prayers he mouthed, automatically, ceaselessly, as he stumbled forward by day, as he fell asleep on frozen ground by night.

Now, so many years later, the boy Andrew rides up on his little sister's pink Care Bears bicycle. He calls the old man "Uncle." Then the sister toddles over to the lawn chair where Anthony sits in the summer sun listening to Portuguese music on the radio and trying to recall war memories which he says are "embedded in your head, mixed up like hamburger." She slaps his bony, protruding knee, as if he has been bad.

Nearby watches the Virgin Mary, in the form of a statuette posed against an upright seashell fringed in blue. It was a present to his mother from the neighbors. Anthony has wrapped the entire thing in plastic. Suddenly he points at the toddler girl and asks, "Would you gas her?" She goes off after her brother. "Wouldn't you save her, if you had the power?"

"If there's a god out there," he continues, "why did he allow those people, babies and ladies, to be gassed if he could have saved them?" For Anthony it is not an academic question—the carnage of war, the suffering of the innocents, the casual brutality of man, the Holocaust. After all these years, he would still like a decent answer. "Apparently he can only do so much," mulls Anthony. Then he adds, "But that's not right. No, there's nothing out there, I really don't think so. I hope I'm wrong, but I don't think I am."

We can be sure of this: Anthony disbelieves not solely because he suffered greatly. He has discarded his faith as an act of charity, to honor the suffering of others. However, he has kept the religion. It's how he was raised, states Anthony, it's what he knows. Also his mother would want him at mass, saying the prayers. And maybe, like he says, he could be wrong about God, you never know for sure.

They were poor. His father went first, leaving Portugal before Antonio Dias was born. His mother stayed behind, running a machine in a silk factory and sewing dresses around the neighborhood. They finally followed when Antonio turned ten, arriving in the port of Boston in 1933. The boy did not speak a word of English, so his parents put him in the first grade with children half his size. He was Anthony Dears now, Diaz thrown overboard at sea, and within a few years he enrolled in vocational school and worked on a farm in West Bridgewater. He tended the corn and milked the cows, chores he had learned in Portugal.

"I got no education at all," says Anthony Dears.

After Pearl Harbor he was drafted by Uncle Sam (he was not yet a citizen and would not be until 1946) and left for Camp Robinson in Arkansas. "It was fun," Anthony says about basic training—a tough farm boy's perspective. The Army gave him classes in reading and writing and then, after his division shipped to North Africa, used him as occasional translator with Portuguese troops. That was okay, too.

He laughs a lot, talking about the war. Not that it was funny, he says, but he laughs anyway. For instance, take the campaign in Anzio, Italy in January of 1944, when over 100,000 American and British soldiers went ashore

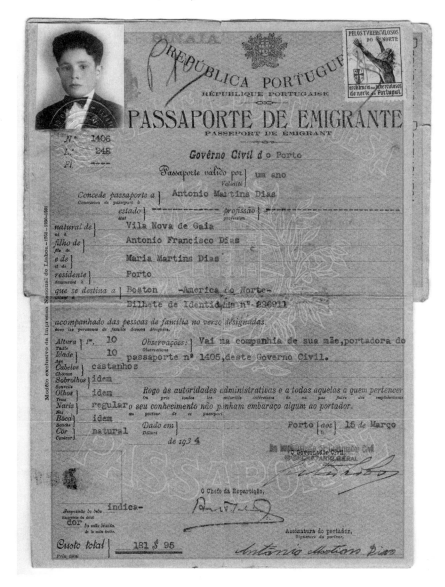

Anthony Dears, then Antonio Francisco Dias, carried this emigration passport on his journey in 1934 from Vila Nova de Gaia in Portugal to the port of Boston, USA. He became a naturalized citizen in 1946.

in the largest amphibian attack of the war to date. Anthony's landing craft stopped short of the beach and dumped him and 20 other guys in water over their heads. The funny thing, or not, was that he had tried to join the Navy earlier and got turned down. Not seaworthy enough, he supposed. He survived because a sergeant grabbed him by the collar and dragged him toward shore.

Then there was the fire fight that got him shot in the back and under his right arm. He thought he was a goner. An awful heat spread over him and he blacked out. Next thing you know, Anthony awoke in a German field hospital with no idea how he had gotten there. He did not know, and has never found out, what happened to the soldiers he fought beside that day. Maybe they were killed, maybe they left him behind thinking he was dead. Either way he woke up, "like I was lost," and became a POW. Somehow, it's good for a sad laugh.

In Stalag 344, where he stayed for nine months, English doctors did their best to treat his wounds. As he slowly healed, Anthony starved. On a meager diet of barley soup and bread, with the odd potato or scrap of horse meat, he worried that his stomach would shrink to a pea and never expand again. The POWs slept on hard boards with no heat and no blankets. When spring came, Anthony found enough strength to play a little softball and it was the craziest thing, the Canadians always seemed to win. By night at 344 he watched American bombers hit the nearby airfield again and again, and he wondered if they would get hit by mistake—especially when the airfield lights were turned off and the camp's were left burning. The guards taunted the prisoners: "You're gonna get bombed tonight!"

But Anthony knew they were scared, too. "They were human beings, I didn't hate them," he says. "They had guns at their backs, too."

Roll calls lasted four to five hours at a time. POWs collapsed from exhaustion and "each time they fell down the guards would hit them with their rifles," stated Anthony in a 1949 affidavit he filed with the U.S. government to gain compensation for what he blandly described as his "mistreatment" and "unpaid labor" in the Stalags. One morning, he testified, all the POWs were taken into a field at dawn after an escape attempt. They stood for six hours in the snow, barely clothed, "machine guns pointed at us from all around the field and we expected any minute that we would be shot."

By and large, captivity was tedious and lonely. At every turn Anthony looked for someone who spoke Portuguese, but always came up dry. For his last three months at the camp he worked all day, every day, cleaning horses and horse barns. In November he was shipped by box car to IIIB, where conditions were even worse. Again there was no heat and the POWs were kept in barracks around the clock. After that he was crated to Stalag IIB, another hell hole. The area of the camp reserved for Allied prisoners, though, was heaven compared to the section where 10,000 Russians were abandoned to die.

Anthony's bizarre, three-month march round and round Nazi Europe began in January of 1945. The POWs were denied food by their guards, so they lived off Red Cross parcels scavenged from the storehouse at IIB and food stolen from the homes of German civilians in the dead of night. "Some

Anthony Dears as a young soldier.

of the prisoners were afraid to do this," states Anthony, "but I was willing to take the chance of being shot for the sake of something to eat." His column slogged about 15 miles per day and he guesses it might have killed him, as it did so many others, if he had not gotten desperate enough to bolt. A farmer gave him the location of the American lines and he just ran like crazy through the woods for hours until he knocked smack into a company of GIs.

So a couple of months later he sat in his kitchen in Brockton, slurping Holy Ghost soup. Like he had never left, on the surface of things. He made sure not to tell his mother he had been wounded until six months passed, and then

Anthony Dears

only because she saw the scars while he washed at the sink. Anthony took a job in a leather factory—he stayed a year, then 29 more—and retired with a pension in 1971 after his father died. He built a house next door for his little brother, a Korean War vet who drank himself to death.

Anthony came close, but never married. "No luck," he says. And all the time he took care of his ma, brought her around to the feasts and sampled the Holy Ghost soups. Each one a little different, and always delicious. He accompanied his ma to church and murmured prayers that he did not believe—on the other hand, he likes to add, you never know for sure.

"I've had a good time, after the war part," he says. "I would have liked to have some kids, but I don't brood about it."

In the side yard, Anthony grows rows of tomatoes. Everything is behind this year because of a hail storm in the spring. Once the tomatoes ripen, he will put them in bags and hang them on the neighbors' fences. Who knows if they will use them, he says, everyone is so busy these days. If they rot, they rot. Anthony also tends a Concord grape arbor and high bush blueberries that taste sharper than sweet, and he is teaching Andrew to grow wavy green scallions in the herb garden, next to the mint. They used to have a pony to fertilize the garden; the boy would have liked that.

An old chestnut tree leans over the grape arbor. It drops "pipe cleaners," tendrils that dangle like earrings from the tips of the branches. The grapes are rotting as they ripen, unfortunately, and Anthony has a theory that it is caused by acid from the pipe cleaners. So he is thinking of cutting down the chestnut. Its leaves are bug-eaten, too. But there is no hurry, and the tree gives good shade to the backyard where the children play and he sits and talks about war.

"It's all about greed," says the old POW, trying to explain why we spend more money on killing than helping. He wishes there was some kind of vaccination against greed, because that is what it might take in the end.

FLIER: EMANUEL REMPELAKIS'S STORY

Emanuel Rempelakis looked up past the guidelines of his blooming parachute and saw the airplane, a burning B-17 bomber, disintegrate. On that day, September 12, 1943, Emanuel did not know that he was the only flier in the ten-man crew to have jumped clear, did not consider that the men, or parts of them, were accelerating past him at terrific speed. Now he drifted through a sunlit German sky, exposed for all the Third Reich to see. A group of children waited below, in a field on the outskirts of Munich.

Emanuel hit the ground hard and the children began to beat him senseless. "Jude, Jude," the Hitler Youth yelled, maybe a dozen of them, 11, 12 years old, chanting "Jew, Jew," because they had been taught to believe everything they were told, and they had been told that the airmen destroying their factories and cities and armies were filthy Jews. So the children fractured his skull, broke his left arm at the elbow, and colored his body with bruises. They slashed his face with a knife and knocked out four teeth.

"They don't know a Greek coming down the parachute," remembers the airman, who, for all the good it did him, was not Jewish but Greek Orthodox. "They hated me like I was the only one bombing the place." That sunny day, Emanuel suffered under the storm of blows until a German policeman arrived. He blew his whistle and roused the boys away.

Only later, after the war, was Emanuel told that his name means "God be with you." That is why you survived, his mother told him. The name she gave him, that is why he did not die from getting shot down three times— three times! That is why partisans smuggled him back from Yugoslavia the first and second times he dived from a burning plane, in February and July of '43, and that is why the good cop chased away the ravenous children, and why, after 16 months in a POW camp, he survived the tortuous Black March at war's end.

That is why. Actually, though, Emanuel does not mean "God be with you." It means "God with us." It is a statement, really, more than a prayer.

Emanuel Rempelakis

So if God was with the cocky young flier—cocky enough to *volunteer* for that last mission, his 51st, hell, he figured, it could not happen a third time —then wasn't God with everyone else, too? Didn't it stand to reason that God stood among the boys in the exploding plane? Wasn't that God in the gutter with the starved and shot-dead POWs he passed on the road during the Black March? Emanuel means "God with us," all of us, so didn't God look up with the Hitler Youth as the American floated down?

At age 84, Emanuel tries not to gnaw over this kind of thing. "I say, forget it," he declares. "I didn't plan to get shot down. It happened, why think about it all the time?"

But the families of the men who disintegrated in the blue sky above his parachute could not forget. They insisted on meeting with Emanuel, in a hotel in Cincinnati. There they asked him why nine-tenths of the crew—flying their first mission, alongside the experienced flight engineer—why did they not make it out of the plane? They wanted to know why *he* did. What happened up there? Didn't he try to help their sons, their husbands? The families demanded answers and Emanuel did his best to describe how he urged the crew out of the plane, yelling "Go! Go! Go!" but they were inexperienced, they froze, and he explained how he had bailed out twice before, so he knew the procedure only too well. That is why he lived, that and dumb luck. But nothing he said could resurrect their beloved boys. Some of the family members became angry and accused him of abandoning the crew.

"It was hell," he says, "but I had to do it."

He did not, of course, tell the grieving families about the name, Emanuel —having that kind of edge did not seem fair. The chance of an Allied flyer surviving 30 missions early in the war, before the German air force was decimated, was about one in three. But surviving 51 missions? And *three* shoot downs? And the Hitler Youth and prison and everything else? Their kids, for god's sake, did not last *one* mission. Those families must have looked at Emanuel as if he had taken all the good luck for himself—as if he had stolen it. So you can see why, certainly, he could not tell them what Emanuel meant.

But then he insists that no one calls him Emanuel, anyway. No one ever did. Friends and family call him Rumpy, or just Greek. As in Hey, Greek, how'd you manage getting shot down all those times? His reply: "You know why I did it? Why I survived all that shit? To collect, that's why!" Chew on that awhile. Rumpy has a good laugh.

Without missing a beat, he explains that he has received disability payments almost from the day he walked on bowed, ruined legs toward American troops advancing across Germany. The checks started at $25 a month. Some POWs turned it down, he says, called it too little, an insult. Not him —that money grew and helped put his kids through college and buy a little place on Cape Cod.

"But I'm still a poor Greek," he adds.

Emanuel gets out his Department of Veterans Affairs paperwork. It is all written down, he says, everything you need to know. While he is at it, he shows off his long medication list, treating conditions that grew from the beating in Munich and from prolonged dysentery and malnutrition in captivity, ailments which persisted as he attended art school and married an Irish girl (to his parents' dismay), as he raised three kids and enjoyed a long career editing trade publications.

The day he parachuted to earth for the third time, however, he had serious doubts about his future. After the beating, and rescue, he was moved to an interrogation center. He cannot remember what happened there. "You'd think I wouldn't be forgetting these things," he says, lamenting memories pulled thin over the decades. "Maybe it's a blessing, so I can sleep at night." Then the Germans threw him in a boxcar with other downed fliers and days later the train arrived at Luft Stalag IV, a camp for Allied airmen.

Although POW camps run by the Luftwaffe were less severe than camps for infantry, Luft Stalag IV was a hard and monotonous place. Emanuel wore the same dirty outfit for 16 months. He walked endlessly about the grounds, despite his injuries. A good talker, he shared stories with airmen from the United States, Britain, and Canada. Rumpy's three shoot downs —no one could beat that! Had to be a World War II record! The camp, surrounded by guard towers and double-barbed wire fences, was nearly escape proof.

There was little medical care, but the Germans did issue equipment for softball. Emanuel played first base. To kill time, he stitched a handkerchief that recorded his bombing missions, using a cadged needle, thread pulled from his socks, and a square of fabric—probably a scrap of silk parachute. The invocation "Hello, Laddies," scrawled in puffy letters, floats across the peculiar artifact now framed in his basement over a desk. Along the adjoining walls hang photos of Emanuel posing with celebrities he met at fancy parties in his days with *Television Week*. Sarah Vaughn, Dinah Shore, even the Three Stooges. "They loved the write-ups," he says—this before *TV Guide* squashed the competition.

The food at Luft Stalag IV, he says, was almost nothing. Hot water for breakfast. Sauerkraut soup for lunch. One potato for dinner. Contrary to news reports fueled by German propaganda, Red Cross parcels were rare and disappeared entirely as Allied bombing increased in 1945. Month by month his body evaporated. Emanuel entered the Army Air Corps at 155 pounds; he weighed all of 82 pounds at liberation. Meanwhile, back home in Boston, his parents lived on hope. The first two times their son had been shot down they received Missing-in-Action telegrams. This time it was the MIA/KIA variety. Killed-in-Action, most likely, because the plane had exploded. Nobody saw a chute. Not until the spring of 1945 did they learn that Emanuel was alive.

Now he takes two photos from his wallet. One is Emanuel as flyboy in aviator shades. The other is Emanuel as immigrant boy, one year old and propped between his parents soon after they arrived at Ellis Island from Sitia, Greece. It was 1922, he thinks, or maybe 1921. The family settled in Boston, in the Roxbury neighborhood with other poor Greeks, Blacks, Jews, and Irish. After school as a teenager, Emanuel manned a soda fountain and delivered papers. His father worked constantly and in time opened three seafood restaurants.

In Luft Stalag IV, Emanuel stitched this record of his bombing missions using a scrounged needle, thread pulled from his socks, and what appears to be a scrap of parachute silk. It was framed in his basement for many years.

"All I know," says Emanuel, "is I never saw him."

As soon as he could, and this was before Pearl Harbor, he enlisted in the Army Air Corps. He wanted his choice of duty, "just in case a war came," and decided to train as a flight engineer, responsible for every system on the plane. He enjoyed sitting up front with the pilots, third in command. A flight engineer is a jack-of-all-trades, says Emanuel proudly, even capable of flying the bird in a pinch. The indispensable man.

It is hard in retirement, though, to stay indispensable. Emanuel spends his days gardening, painting, and shooting photographs, and he often takes to the garage to make birdhouses and shelves for the neighbors in his condo community. As long as they pay for the wood, that is; they cannot have

Emanuel Rempelakis as a young soldier.

the shelves without paying. His garage is filled with boxes of souvenirs from his days with a beverage industry magazine. Key rings, hats, t-shirts, pens— he likes handing them out, especially to ex-POW buddies.

"You have to keep active," Emanuel says, to last a long time. Survival is a family trait. His dad lived to 98, his mom to 99.

On February 6, 1945, the POWs of Luft Stalag IV were marched out of camp. Hitler was pulling the prisoners closer to Berlin, perhaps as bargaining chips in peace negotiations, perhaps to kill them in a final murderous act. For the next 86 days, Emanuel and several thousand POWs marched

600–800 miles through freezing temperatures and snow storms. Most nights they slept outdoors. There was little to eat, except what they scavenged from farms or were given by German civilians. And if you stopped for long, you would get a whack on the head for your trouble. As if that was not bad enough, how about a bomb in the kisser from your own air force—maybe from one of the guys you used to know. Emanuel recalls diving off the road, explosions all around, torn bodies everywhere. Day after day, for what seemed forever.

Hundreds of men died of illness and starvation on the Black March, and many were shot when they dropped out of the line. Some men struggled on homemade crutches. Emanuel prayed to God over and over as he slogged forward, through "a horror show." It was tough beyond belief and that is why, he says, he could get on with life when he returned. Like the wife says, nothing ever bothers you. Not after that.

But some people still do not believe it, he says, wearily. They think he is making it all up. And they have the cockeyed idea from movies and TV shows like *Hogan's Heroes* that life for POWs was cushy, not a battle for

Emanuel Rempelakis

survival. He has even been asked about German girls. What were they like? Did you get laid?

Emanuel shakes his head in disgust. There is one group of women he does remember, with incredible vividness. He remembers women behind the barbed wire of a concentration camp that he passed on the Black March. It may have been Ravensbruk, where 92,000 women died, or the camp at Wobbelin. He remembers the women climbing the fence, screaming, and he remembers the calm hatred of his German guards. They said, "Forget it, don't even look at them." Emanuel remembers children screaming alongside the women, too. Was God there, too, with those kids?

"Oh my, the things I saw," says Emanuel. He shakes his head again, and then changes the subject. It is a terrible wonder, all the things Emanuel and God saw.

Emanuel Rempelakis died in September 2005. It began with a fall, a bailout strangely enough, appropriately enough, just three months earlier. He tripped on a shoe, he told his wife Mary. When he hit the ground, his hip broke, and then the doctors found prostate cancer and his heart grew weaker and weaker and it all went downhill from there. He endured an operation to relieve a subdural hematoma and finally succumbed to a stroke, the final blow.

Months earlier Emanuel had received notification that he was awarded the Distinguished Flying Cross from the U.S. Air Force, given to flyers who have demonstrated, according to the citation, "Heroism or extraordinary achievement in aerial flight." The medal arrived at the house after he died and is cherished by his family.

CHAPTER 8

Dark Passages

MANNA FROM HEAVEN: BERNARD TRAVERS'S STORY

At Kommando 64B, in the early spring of 1945, the Germans put them to work building roadblocks for tanks. The cement recipe called for three parts sand, one part concrete, but the POWs mixed at a six to one ratio. Bernard Travers imagined tank shells exploding the roadblocks as if they were sandcastles. Now and then the men broke a shovel, lost a crowbar. "Our way of being saboteurs," says Bernard, an American infantryman captured five months earlier on night patrol in northern France.

A bunch of them even escaped one evening through an opening they cut in a barbed-wire fence. Walking through fields, exhausted from hunger and punishing work, they watched bomb flashes break the darkness as Berlin burned to the south. They wore filthy clothes and packed no guns or ID papers. But it was the Big Escape—they were out, on their own, free.

"Now where do we go?" one POW asked. None of them knew how to read the stars. Where are the Germans, the Russians, the Americans? Will Allied forces liberate the camp while we wander this godforsaken country, practically asking to be shot? The sky flashed to the south. Eventually the men turned around and went back to their cage; the guards did not even know they had left.

Weeks later they were marched out of 64B and put in a thick column of POWs, German soldiers, and refugees—the world in flight, to the west and away from the ravaging Russian army that spent its own soldiers like bullets. They marched for five days, for over 100 miles, as artillery pounded the earth and British planes dove low and strafed the roads, no questions

Bernard Travers

asked. Bernard saw German MPs pull deserters from the column and shoot them. Without proper papers, you were shot. "Everyone had to have papers," he says.

On the fifth day of the march, American infantry troops came down the road. Now all tables were turned. Guards transformed into prisoners, the judged rose up into judges. In the garden of an opera house, where the

POWs slept, Bernard watched a "striped gang" of six Holocaust survivors beat a German to death. It took that many, they were so near death themselves. The German wore brown pants and shiny black boots, somewhere between civilian clothes and a military uniform. The survivors cried, "What happened to my mother? Where is my father?"

Bernard felt the impulse to stop them. He could not do it. "They were guilty only of justice," he says and then right away, as if it is the natural ending to the story, he talks about a woman he met earlier on the march, a young mother pushing a toddler in a baby carriage. He gave her a can of dried milk from a Red Cross package—called Klim, backwards for milk—and tried to explain, with hand gestures and a little German, how to twist the key to open the can and how to mix the powder with water. How to make Klim.

Bernard does not remember the mother's reaction. "There's no face, no features, I only see these shapes." But he is glad, very glad, that he had the chance to give Klim to the mother and child on that dangerous road.

"I love children," he says. He has three of his own, and a couple of grand-children in Florida. In fact, he would like to move down there but his wife claims that packing would kill her, and she is probably right. He opens a kitchen cupboard stuffed with papers and containers and long-ago, crammed-together belongings. "It's like that all over the place," he sighs.

Bernard Travers's ancestors arrived from Ireland in the 1840s, during the Great Potato Famine. He was born in 1924 in Boston in the low-rent flat-lands at the base of Mission Hill, but his family did well enough to own a telephone, an automobile, and a summer cottage built by his dad. When money got tight in the '30s, Bernard shoveled snow, set pins at a bowling alley, and caddied for 75 cents a round. Top it off with a quarter tip, he recalls, "and you're in Heaven."

At Catholic schools, the Notre Dame nuns and Xaverian brothers taught Bernard about the genuine article, Heaven Above—open to all God's children in the Universal Church of believers in Jesus Christ. He attended Boston College in 1942 as the first member of his family to go to college—his two older sisters were shunted to secretarial school—and he commuted to class by hitchhiking or riding the backs of street cars to avoid the fare. Nights he worked behind the meat counter of a grocery store. Soon after getting his call-up papers in the spring—goodbye student, hello soldier—Bernard was summoned to receive rosary beads and a pat on the back from one of the deans, a Jesuit priest. "First and last time I ever saw him," he laughs.

This was America, after all, so the military gave him a choice: Army, Navy, or Marine Corps? Bernard chose Army, and they chose for him gunner in the Army Air Corps. It was an assignment true to rumored form: WASPs flew the planes, Jews navigated, and the Irish and Italians manned

Bernard Travers carried these rosary beads throughout the war. They were given to him by a Jesuit priest at Boston College on the day Bernard left school for the Army.

the guns. Lucky for him, though, he was a Joe College Irish boy, and new orders sent him to Lehigh University to join the Army Student Training Program. The big idea was to mold an elite corps that, at war's end, would rebuild a devastated world. Given one more choice, Bernard picked dental and languages for his specialty. They slotted him for engineering.

"You chased girls, you enjoyed life," he says. "Those were marvelous times." As for the war, "It's over there, it's *them,* like viewing a far vista or a stage play." But soon the vista slammed forward; the play seized you for an actor; and Bernard found himself face down in the Louisiana mud, just another infantry grunt. He was shipped to England in August of 1944.

"They needed bodies," he states. "You go where the list sends you, don't ask why."

The list sent him into combat in Northern France. "It became real," says Bernard. "You lived for the next sound you heard." A shell decapitated two men next to him. He stepped on a Bouncing Betty land mine that did not explode. In silent moments Bernard gripped the dean's rosary and murmured prayers. Back home his mother was praying, too. But not for his survival. She prayed that he would not kill anyone, as if more concerned with his soul than his life.

Nothing so theological for Bernard. He wanted to live and prayed for that, period. Did he kill anyone? Well, there is no record of it. He never saw the enemy until he was captured on a night patrol, but you did not have to see someone to kill him. All you had to do was fire your gun in the direction you were told.

"Your feet are not on the same earth as they used to be," he describes his existence after the capture. "I was an automaton. If someone said jump, I'd jump; stop, I'd stop." Bernard strapped his Movado watch, a present from his parents, to his genitals in order to have something to trade. In the German towns of Duisberg and Essen, women and older men came out to curse and spit at the POWs. *"Terrorfliegers,"* they shouted, believing they were downed airmen, the cruel ones from on high.

In Essen, the strangest thing happened. Bernard saw an intact building that he recognized, vaguely, from home. "Like a stroke," it hit him. How could I be here and there at the same time? Is all the world merging in this conflagration? Years later Bernard walked past City Hall in Cambridge, Massachusetts, US of A, and realized—that is the building! Again like a stroke, there and here.

The POWs were loaded in boxcars, like cattle—like Jews, he would learn in time—and they began a halting journey without food or water or elbow room. In four days they arrived at Stalag XIB in Fallingbostel. "A dreary, foreboding place," says Bernard, "where the sky never seemed to turn blue." The men were confined for 23 hours per day, and from a window in his barracks Bernard gazed at the woods beyond the fence and dreamed of Sherman tanks breaking through the pine trees, knocking them down like Popsicle sticks.

His dreams, very quickly, segued from tanks to food. Their daily ration: ersatz coffee or tea; a small bowl of cabbage broth; and bread with sawdust in the mix, from a loaf to be divided between seven men. Each of the seven men took one day per week to do the cutting, and the cutter got the last slice. If the Nazis believed that throwing loaves to the wolves would create discord, set the strong against the weak, they were wrong. The men cooperated. Occasionally, Bernard scrounged a seed potato or a string of meat "like a shoelace." He lost 50 pounds in captivity.

The POWs concocted elaborate recipes, sugary and filled with longing, and pronounced them out loud like prayers. Candy was Bernard's favorite ingredient, candy dripping in meat, potatoes, everything. Their actual

Bernard Travers as a young soldier.

diet—he has looked it up, it is a fact—was similar to what victims in concentration camps received.

At Christmastime, he was moved by boxcar to Stalag 2A at Neubrandenburg, near the North Sea. For the first time Red Cross parcels began to arrive and the world narrowed to their contents: prunes or raisins, chocolate, instant coffee, vitamin C pills, packs of cigarettes, Klim, and Swan soap. British POWs taught Bernard to concoct "duff" made from barley, raisins, Klim, and water. He used thread from the hem of his coat to repair his socks—a tiny assertion, moving thread from one place to another.

You needed to do little things like that, to call your own, because "a POW camp makes a man a robot," Bernard says. What to eat, when to go to the bathroom, all decided for you. Even the friendships he made with other

POWs could not be sustained, as men died or were moved from camp to camp in the last, churning months of the war. Bernard describes it as a process of "endless stripping"—of your body, of status, of the warmth you carried inside. People disappeared, one by one, and you did not want to get too close, did not want to have your anxious heart stripped away, too.

Even to this day, "I'm within myself," he says, but this he accepts. You can still make a life. The liberated Bernard finished school at Boston College, raised a family, and sold scaffolding for buildings and insurance for 30 years. Yes, he was a solitary whiskey drinker, but not a recluse. Bernard chatted and laughed with thousands of customers. And yet always there was the business at hand, the papers on the table between him and the other person.

Stalag 2A had a church. Bernard managed to slip free and attend a few times. A French priest said mass in Latin, and once he gave Bernard an extra ration of bread. "Manna from heaven," he remembers with fervor. On Easter Sunday, the Germans allowed anyone in the camp to attend. Prisoners took turns reading passages of the Gospel in several languages—English, French, German, Italian, maybe Russian or Polish—and as the alien languages crowded the church in layer after layer of scripture, of death and resurrection, Bernard thought of the Notre Dame nuns at The Lady of Perpetual Help Grammar School. He thought of how they spoke about the Universal Church.

"We're all the same," the nuns used to say, but of course they meant all Catholics, perhaps all Christians on a good day. Bernard does not keep to such nonsense. Everyone's the same the world over, he says—but most of all in the way that we hate each other, in our capacity to destroy.

"We all have that urge to destruction," says the man who gave the mother and child his last can of Klim. "It's been that way for thousands of years and it's not going to change."

STARING AT THE SKY: VIT KRUSHAS'S STORY

"I don't want to come back as a human," Vit told Dr. Kuderaskis, a Veterans Affairs psychiatrist who specialized in treating former POWs. "I'd probably choose a squirrel. I've tried to keep them out of my bird feeder for 40 years."

Dr. Kuderaskis died about six years ago. Vit's wife, Anna, died last November of uterine and lung cancer—he smoked, she didn't, how do you like that—and a sister went earlier in the year. And then it was David Brudnoy, the radio talk master who Vit listened to every night, from cancer and AIDS.

"It's been a helluva year," he says.

Theresa LeVasseur.
Box 424
Caribou, Maine

THIS SIDE OF CARD IS FOR ADDRESS

Miss M. ——
4 Higgusworth St.
Roxbury Mass.

Dear Miss   Jan. 24, 1945
    I just had to write to tell you about Bernard Travers.
He is now a prisoner of war in Germany according to
German radio broadcast I heard tonight. I know you'll
be happy to know he is allright. His message read on
the broadcast read as follows: Dear M--- I am a prisoner of war-- I am well and happy-- Regards to all your
family-- Love from Bernard--- ASN 31310479
    I am 15 yrs. old and live in northern Maine. I would
deeply appreciate any answer from you. I hope and pray
your loved one returns to you safely after this war.
May he be in safety until then. I have two brothers in
the service- One in the So. Pacific and the other is i
the states as yet. So we know how it is to be separate
from ones who are so dear to us. God Bless You
                           Goodnight
                 Theresa LeVasseur.

Theresa LeVasseur, a member of a ham radio club, heard Bernard Travers's name on a German radio broadcast listing the names of POWs. The 15-year-old girl, whose brothers were away in the service, sent this heartfelt postcard from her home in remote Caribou, Maine, to Bernard's family in Roxbury, Massachusetts.

This is the first time he has lived alone, ever. You would think that would be awful for Vitold Krushas, but he denies it, says he has always been a loner, always took to the woods by himself to be among the trees and streams and wildlife, to get in the canoe and do a little fishing. On New

Vit Krushas

Year's Day he would slip into a pine grove and listen to the Orange Bowl on his transistor, to the faraway crowd cheering football heroes. And at home, too, he holed up in his musty basement, smoking his pipe. Hour after hour, sitting in a lawn chair on the dirt floor of the basement where no one else liked to be, Vit listened to the family shuffling overhead.

He tells this story about his wife, Anna, the woman he wrote to 60 years ago from an air base in England asking her to be his girl. The woman who wrote back with a simple yes. You see, their oldest son Kenny, serving in Vietnam, was blown out of a tank and nearly died. Then younger brother Peter opened his draft notice. Enough was enough for Anna. She got on the phone with a military official—her husband, she told him, held prisoner in Germany. Her Kenny, shattered. And now you want my Peter? Do you want our dog, too? Vit remembers her yelling into the phone. Do you want our beagle for a squad dog? Instead of Vietnam, Peter received duty on the DMZ in Korea.

Vit looks ahead to the spring, when he and his two sons will set Anna's ashes into the columbarium. "We'll go together if I'm dead by then," he says without much conviction, and then laments his polymyalgia and his lack of energy for shoveling snow and cutting grass, for fishing and digging in the garden. (He stopped hunting 20 years ago. "I'd had enough of killing," he says.) Vit maintains that he has aged too quickly over the last few months —as if it were some mean trick, not letting him ease into it. Just boom, everything changed.

Now, as if to compensate, he looks back to another era when all the neighbors were poor and he rode his bike down to the Brockton Airport and stared at the sky as the biplanes and Taylor Cubs came in for landings. Back to when he had one toy, that's it, a cast-iron airplane, and back to when he devoured pulp magazines like *Daredevil Aces* and *Sky Fighter,* and when he was the ace shot on the rifle club and worked construction for the Common Laborers and Hod Carriers Union—top wages, 80 cents an hour. He remembers when everything was cheaper and they used newspaper for toilet paper and did not care. Even the pinball scores were lower back then.

"I'd love to go through those days again," he says. Everything was better, before the war.

Vit endured eleven months as a POW at Stalag 17B in Krems, Austria, and then survived an 18-day, westward march away from the Russian juggernaut—a journey taking him to the gates of Mauthausen concentration camp, to the maw of death— but first he had to get shot from the sky.

It happened this way. April 29, 1944: the *San Antone Rose* crossed the English Channel on a daylight run, its eighth mission, although only five were actually recorded in the Bomber Command books. Mechanical problems had sent Vit and crew home on three missions without dropping their bombs; tough luck, fellas, no bombs, no credit. Thirty-one complete missions bought a ticket home, a long-shot outcome at this stage of the war. Vit was a waist gunner—dream job for a kid who loved guns and planes— and on this day he was one of thousands of gunners in 751 bombers thundering toward the Friedrichstrasse Railroad Station north of Berlin. The flak was pretty thick—you had to fly right through it—when 50 German fighter planes came in rows of ten out of the sun.

"Like a flock of blackbirds," says Vit.

Now if you want a primer on how to operate a waist gun, how the bullets come out of the muzzle and hit walls of streaming air, how to gauge angles and firing radiuses and what deflection shooting means, then Vit's your man. He had trained for months, he was top-class. But on that day it did not matter, and it still bothers Vit, the crack rifle-club shot, the kid who could spatter a squirrel at 40 yards, that he could not protect the plane. In seconds his right 50mm and its elevation motor were shot up. He could see the German pilots just off the wing tips. There was nothing he could do.

The plane burned wing tip to wing tip, says Vit, "aluminum peeling off like wax paper," and below him the fuel tanks—"they looked like

Vit Krushas as a young soldier.

coffins"—burst afire. Vit knew they were going to their deaths, and the only way out was through the open bomb-bay doors. The bombs were stuck there—so this was not a real mission, it did not count toward the magic number—and they were on fire, too. Vit slapped on his parachute but the damn thing was upside down and covered with burning fuel, and he struggled to get it latched right. Then he leaned forward, 25,000 feet over Hamburg, Germany, and fell.

Like those poor people falling from the World Trade Center on 9/11, he says. Fire everywhere, you gotta leave. Impossible to stay. Vit just let go and dropped between the burning bombs and out the bay doors, and his flak helmet blew off in the slipstream. For a moment he thought his head had been cut off, but then realized that he was thinking, so his head was attached after all. So he was not dead. Still, he imagined his mother holding the KIA telegram and, funny thing, at the same time he remembered the weather report (clouds 7/10 at 12,000 feet) and as Vit hit cloud—upside down, feet heavenward—he popped the chute and the impact snapped him eight-feet long. His float down seemed to take ages, a lifetime between sky and earth, and at one point a Me-109 fighter appeared. Vit hung loose, as if dead. The plane swerved away.

Finally, approaching fast, he saw "a golden field, yellow from early spring" and he landed in a tree with one of the chute cords wrapped like a noose around his neck. He blacked out. That was it.

Lucky for Vit, a German man cut him down from the tree. He awoke to a new world. His savior wore a civil-defense hat and let Vit lean on his bicycle as they moved along. He took the American flier home to show his family—an autistic child wandered the back yard, the wife had a sister in Boston—and Vit wondered if this wasn't his lucky day. Maybe they would hide him. Maybe he had found the underground. Then the Nazis arrived, very business like, and several days later Vit stepped off a boxcar and walked into Stalag 17B, a prison for noncommissioned officers and less-than-human Russians. Previously, it had been a concentration camp for Polish undesirables.

All his life, Vit says, he lived on hot dogs, hot dogs, hot dogs. Oh boy, those jumbo dogs from Howard Johnson's restaurant, he would bike an hour for one of those! At Stalag 17B it was rutabaga or potato soup for lunch, with maggots like grains of rice. For breakfast and dinner, hot water. Red Cross parcels were infrequent. During his year of captivity, Vit withered from 165 to 100 pounds, and come winter the fragile, shivering POWs burned tar paper from the barracks walls for heat. Roll calls were constant, day or night, sun or sleet, and the camp was surrounded with two barbed-wire fences charged with electricity. A deadline wire had been strung inside the fences; step over the line, you're dead.

During delousing, as their clothes baked in ovens to kill the vermin, the POWs took showers under pipes dripping cold water and used soap that did not lather, soap made from murdered human bodies.

But still, it was not always awful. They had their moments. At night the POWs played poker, the games lit by socks filled with butter they acquired from trading cigarettes with the guards. POWs had the better cigarettes—Avalons, Wings, and Red Dogs for poker or trading with other prisoners. Old Golds and Camels for greasing the palms of Germans. A batch of Camels fetched radio parts, and for awhile the POWs even managed a tunnel between the American and Russian compounds.

Vit once swapped a stack of cigarette packs for a Swiss Army knife. He figured it was a sweet deal for the Russian, a useless knife for a good smoke before you died. He does not say much else about camp life. It felt like a dull ache, with the occasional respite. In October of 1944, for instance, an escape artist known as the Grey Ghost came to 17B and stayed one day before breaking out. At least that was how Vit heard it. And he has a good laugh remembering a man who made a bird trap and caught a squirrel instead—the size of a grasshopper! It was starving, too.

In early April, the POWs were marched out of 17B in groups of 500, as Russian artillery sounded from the east. Vit had kept active in the camp, even as he starved, so the daily 20-mile march was not excruciating for him. The big problem was scrounging for food, scraps, anything to fill your stomach. As the days passed Vit could not help marveling at the beauty of the Austrian countryside, and the deer bounding across clearings reminded him of the Green Mountains of Vermont where he had hunted. At the same time, men were dying of illness and starvation all around him, and some POWs who ran from the column were killed by civilians or German patrols.

One day, as they tromped uphill, the POWs were directed to look at the house where Adolf Hitler was born. There was nothing special about it. A house like all the rest. Another day, as the column moved into Breneau Woods, Vit encountered a little Bavarian boy in front of an Alpine house. The boy carried a "beautiful engraved knife," he remembers, inlaid with a swastika. In the steel were carved the words "Blut und Ehre." Blood and Honor, the SS motto. That night an SS storm trooper held the muzzle of a submachine gun to Vit's face and accused him of stealing a can of food.

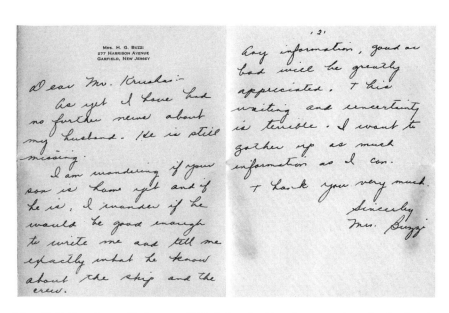

Mrs. H.G. Buzzi sent this letter to Vit's father, looking for news about her husband, Lt. Harold Buzzi, who flew on the *San Antone Rose* when it was shot down in 1944. Harold was one of five crew members killed that day; Vit and four others jumped clear and became POWs.

Vit and his group of POWs noticed dead bodies along the road. This was days later, perhaps. Then more and more bodies, "like rocks in the fields," he says, and the road turned from dirt to white powder. A yellow-green smoke fouled the air. It smelled—and this could have been my imagination, says Vit—like burnt human flesh. Then he saw the smokestacks and the high fence and the huge gates with the Nazi eagle over it. Through the fence he saw windows on the barracks and in those windows he saw skeletal heads looking out, screaming. Maybe the poor souls imagined we would liberate them, Vit wonders. That we would storm the place and take them to another world. That we were soldiers again.

The march halted. A German officer stood at the gates of Mauthausen. Smiling, he pointed at the POWs and swept his arm inward. Come in, you're invited. What, nobody interested? Then Vit turned around and watched as a work party of Jews moved double-time down the road, returning to camp. Heads shaved, in black-and-white pajamas, they were all "staring at the sky," he recalls, "skin pulled over their bones, reaching for God, for food, grabbing at birch twigs and trying to eat them."

Then, "the worst thing." The thing that if you did not let it change you, you were not human. Vit saw two Jews helping a comrade along, holding him up between them. The man had no teeth, no kneecaps, and his dead legs dragged, "making grooves in the road." Finally, his friends could not carry him any longer and he dropped away. An SS man, like a vulture, pulled out his gun and shot the man right there on the ground. They left him behind.

Vit cried, as he cries now. The German guard next to him cried. They spent 30 minutes at Mauthausen, no more, and then continued on their way.

The American flag saved them once, says Vit. On a straight road, just out of the mountains, a P-47 roared down and strafed the column. POWs and guards jumped into the brush; several men were hit. On the second pass, a couple of POWs unfurled the American flag and used it to signal the plane. It veered away, tipping its wings.

"It's a hell of a lot more than a symbol," states Vit, and with startling anger he criticizes a girl at a local high school who turned her back on the flag during an assembly, her way of protesting the war in Iraq. He is reluctant to admit that it may have taken some courage for the girl to do such a thing. What would she and Vit, who glimpsed hell, say to each other if they sat down together?

The march ended at a prison camp north of Breneau, Austria, and the POWs built lean-tos from pine logs. It was cold and snowing, but still Vit noticed the buds showing on the tips of tree limbs, the buds so fragile and dusted white in the first days of May. And he spied, days later as he scooped water from a river, white-starred tanks in the distance.

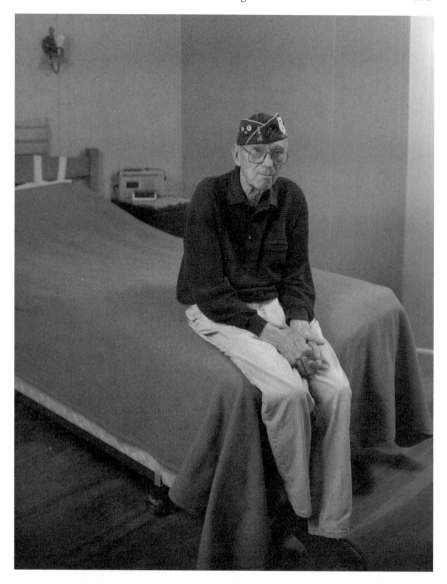

Vit Krushas

"Patton's here!" he cried. "Patton's here!"

While Anna stayed in the hospital for the last time, volunteers from their church renovated the Krushas' living room. So now the walls are painted soft green and the moldings and baseboards are cut sharp and snug. The wood floor is lacquered to a shine. A pyramid of logs, constructed by Vit to burn for hours, glows in the new granite fireplace. Anna loved fireplaces, but did not live to see the final product.

"We never imagined we wouldn't get her home," he says.

In the critical care unit Vit got in the habit of staring at his wife's heart monitor. He would watch the line go up and down, up and down, and he thought about how he had suffered from a "runaway heart" as a young man with a family to support on a machinist's salary, and how he had learned to calm his heart by holding his breath, by keeping the frantic present and ugly past out of himself. So Vit tried that sometimes, at her bedside, holding his breath so Anna's heart would calm. The nurses had to turn off the heart monitor because it was upsetting him too much.

There is too much space, not enough furniture in this renovated room. Not enough stuff collecting ages of dust. It has been, like he says, a hell of a year. So many loved ones gone and no energy to shovel snow or dig in the garden. Skinny as a sapling, Vit folds into his chair. He smokes a pipe and tells his war stories. All the while a black-and-white cat they adopted years ago, named Kitty, comes and goes as she pleases.

Vit Krushas continued to lose weight over the next 13 months. He died of a stroke in December 2005 and now his ashes have been placed next to Anna's.

THE WISE GUY: FRANK MOLINARI'S STORY

Louie Nigro saved his life, that's what matters, but first it helps to know what kind of life he saved.

Frank Molinari grew up in a poor Italian neighborhood in East Cambridge, his dad a pick-and-shovel man gone 12 hours a day, seven days a week. His family lived cheek by jowl to a poultry house where folks pulled live chickens from coops for the slaughtering. Freight trains roared by yards from his bedroom window, shaking the window panes. Frank worked up a pretty good tough-guy swagger, too, no denying that, but not because he felt deprived. His world busted with adventure, swayed to sweet sounds.

He was Speed, because he could not run fast. His friends sported names like Jumbo, Bomber, and Chi-chi. His brother with the whiffle cut, Flathead. No one went by their real name in those days. On Warren Street, they played stickball and relivio and rolled tires in front of passing cars. Or hopped on the bumpers, like rodeo cowboys. Every winter Frank remembers horses tripping on the slippery cobblestones, breaking their legs and having to be shot right there.

Out front of Packey Walsh's bar, Frank shined shoes for drunks, bootleggers, and thieves. Once he polished a pair for Tip O'Neil, when the Speaker was just a local pol, and he ran numbers for the bookies and learned to

Frank Molinari

swear like a man. Fist fights were common, but it was always one-on-one, no guns or knives, and then you shook hands and forgot about it.

There were rules back then, says Frank.

In card games they bet with matchbooks scooped from the gutter. Twenty-five points for the Windsor Hotel—that was a rare one. And nothing beat soaking up 78s in the sound booths at Krey's Music Shop or playing hooky to hear Artie Shaw, Gene Cooper, and the big bands at the RKO Boston. Or sneaking into the old Howard Theater to see the burlesque show. On summer evenings, Frank and his buddies stood on the street corner and sang a cappella. A kid with a harmonica—his father was a deaf-mute—set the key, and they let loose till their parents whistled them home. "I could hear it a mile away," Frank says about his mother's whistle.

"I didn't realize there was a Depression," admits the former POW. "It was a fun world, a good world, not the hatred you got out there now." Right behind his house the train blurs past—at rush hour, every six minutes. The worst part is the chain link fence crowned with barbed wire that the Mass Bay Transit Authority erected between his backyard and the tracks. Frank cut the wire—something he had wanted to do in the POW camps, cut the goddamn wire—but they sent men out and strung it back it up. They won, he says, the government won. So he does not go back there much, his own backyard. His voice is soft, resigned. Dark brown sunglasses hide his eyes.

After high school Frank worked as an apprentice welder at the Charlestown Navy Yard, doing time before the big tap on the shoulder. He clicks off the day he was drafted, March 29, 1943, not long after he got in a beef with the yard commandant. Funny how that works. A million drill steps later and it is the fall of 1944. Army-hard Corporal Frank Molinari—now christened Moe—found himself churning the North Atlantic on the *Aquitania*. "Everyone was heaving their guts out," he says. One day he went on deck for a smoke and the sky had turned green. That's a funny-colored sky, he wondered. He had never seen a sky like that back in the old neighborhood.

The giant wave knocked him flat, and he would have been sea bait if he had not grabbed a hatch. It was, he says, the first time in his life that he felt overwhelming fear.

The second time did not wait: December 1944, standing night guard in the Ardennes Forest in Belgium. Frank heard a metallic clink, clink, clink and the faint hum of heavy engines. Don't sweat it, he had been told, the Germans are broadcasting tank sounds to spook them. You're in a quiet corner of the war, you've got it made. But Frank did not know what to think. The world seemed to be turning out there, coming unglued, and that night in the blank-slate darkness he saw everything imaginable rolling his way. "Elephants, freight trains," he says, "you name it."

The next day Germany launched the massive attack that began the Battle of the Bulge. "Shells bursting in the forest, trees falling down on us, it was like murder," says Frank. One buddy came to him holding up his arm, the hand gone. "I'm scared, Moe," he said. "Where the hell's your hand?" asked Moe, hands do not just disappear, and only then did the poor kid really understand what was missing and he fell dead away.

Frank Molinari as a young soldier.

After several days of fighting, ammo exhausted, a colonel surrendered the troops. They walked down a hillside, rifles held over their heads. For taking that walk, for not dying, Frank tells it straight: "I've been called yellow, a coward, by my own friends when I came home." German frontline soldiers took cigarettes off the Americans, but left each man a few. Seemed a decent thing to do—maybe the krauts weren't so bad. And then, God knows why, the new POWs were put to work filling in tank tracks with snow.

"I'm digging and up comes an arm," he says. This one with a hand, but no body attached to it. Frank swore loudly, attracting the attention of a U.S. Army chaplain. He swore, too, a blue streak like the men back in East Cambridge. "I should have known, the way he talked," states Frank. That should have been the tip-off, he thinks. The chaplain went into a nearby

shed and did not come out. Another U.S. soldier went in and also did not
come out. Finally, Frank was ordered to the shed.

He could not believe his eyes. The chaplain and the soldier had changed
into the uniforms of German officers. There was a third officer, too, and in
good English they urged Frank to take off his jacket and get warm next to
the stove. He said no; something told him to say no. They offered him food;
he said no again. Then the world finished turning over and stopped in a new
and far uglier place. The German who had impersonated a chaplain, like it
was a part in a play, put his pistol to Frank's head. "They're gonna kill
me," he thought.

Maybe they should have, he has often wondered. At gunpoint the German
forced Frank to perform oral sex on one of the officers. After that they beat
him until he lost consciousness.

When he awoke he was strapped to a table, face down, and a beer bottle
had been shoved far up his rectum. The officers were laughing and joking,
speaking in German now, and Frank screamed and screamed and screamed.
Some time later they threw him outside, another carcass, and he bled pro-
fusely into the snow. It seemed so unreal. It could not be happening. The frozen hand, the shed in the woods, the Army chaplain. The beer bottle full of
his own blood.

That is when Louie Nigro appeared. A married man with three kids back
home in Arlington, Massachusetts, Louie was a quiet, somber guy, a private
to Frank's corporal, but older and smarter and not a hothead. Not a sharpie,
not the kind of guy who would have run with Frank and his kind. Now
Louie knelt down next to the crumpled boy. Hey Moe, what happened?
Frank would not tell him. His blood-soaked pants were plastered to his legs.
He tried, but could not walk. So Louie picked the soldier up, out of the red
snow. He carried him, with the help of other POWs, for six days as they
were marched east in the freezing cold.

At the end of that journey, Frank awoke next to a warm stove in some
kind of hall. POWs sprawled everywhere and, weirdly, there was a Christmas tree across the room. Louie was feeding him a hot liquid. He tried one
more time. What happened, Moe? Frank shook his head, and right there
Louie pledged never to ask again.

"The wise guy that I was, that all left me," says Frank. "The only one I
could trust was Louie. He watched over me like he was my father."

At Stalag 4B, the POWs were stripped for delousing. Frank refused, but
Louie gently helped him remove his clothes, peeling the fabric from the
caked blood and over the tender, purple bruises. Stay close, said Louie, do
what I say. He made sure to rip off Frank's corporal stripes, because the
Germans were separating the corporals from the privates. Soon they were
put to work clearing rubble from bombed-out homes and factories in a
nearby town. Louis gave his warm coat to Frank and took the boy's thin
jacket for himself. "I ain't gonna make it," said Frank. "We're both gonna

make it," said Louie, and he told him again and again, keep moving, that's the trick.

POWs are cargo, and grunt labor, and little else. They were shipped to a satellite camp near the Czech border, where for months they broke stones for a railroad bed. They slept in a beer hall, and everyone doubled up to share body heat under two blankets. One morning Frank watched a POW awaken to find that the man next to him, inches away, had died in the night. Days started with four o'clock a.m. roll call. "Always counting us," remembers Frank, "counting us forever." On Sundays they got potato soup with dill, which was supposed to shrink your stomach so you would feel full. Some men were so hungry they stole bread from their brothers, and the guards got their kicks holding kangaroo courts and staging fights between accuser and accused. One time Frank swore at a guard and was put in a tin box, out in the cold for 24 hours. He returned hating everyone, except Louie.

Frank shrunk by a third, under a hundred pounds. Over and over Louie told him, "When we get home, you're coming to my house. Meredith is making ravioli." So they dreamed of pasta and sauce and meat and a woman cooking at a stove. At the cusp of spring, a messenger arrived from the heavens in the form of a Colonel who bailed from his plane and floated down near the camp. He was brought inside and told the POWs to hold on, that the war was winding down. He said, don't be ashamed. You slowed the Germans at the Bulge, you made a difference. The POWs stood a little straighter.

In April of 1945 the camp was liberated by American troops. Halftracks pulled down the fences and the walls of the buildings, good riddance. After a few weeks at a rehabilitation camp, Frank and Louie sailed for home on a hospital ship, the seas as placid as the Charles River. Aboard ship, Frank informed an intelligence officer about the beatings, but not the sexual abuse. There was a limit to what you could tell.

"You brought that on yourself," the officer told the corporal, with surprising disdain. He was referring to the beatings, of course, but all of it hung in the air subject to condemnation. He threatened Frank with a transfer to Alabama, and then to the Pacific War, if he didn't clam up. The officer produced a piece of paper. Sign it, he told Frank. The document, a Security Certificate prepared by Military Intelligence Service, bound him not to speak about his experiences. Frank remembers being told that if he spoke to the press, it would be under pain of 20 years behind wire—American wire.

We don't want the American people thinking that kind of thing happened, the officer told him. Frank did not understand. Why not? They were Nazis, weren't they? It's a war, terrible things happen to people in war—things you could never imagine, even to tough American soldiers, the heroes of the newsreels. Frank did not care what the American people thought and he knew nothing about politics, about the New Germany or the Soviet

On an outing at Revere Beach in 1945, Frank Molinari (left) poses with Ella Marino, his future wife; a girl everyone called Tootsie; and Eddie Klerowski, a childhood friend of Frank's.

Threat. All he knew was what happened. But he signed. Most of all, Frank just wanted to go home.

"I hate them for it," he says. "They forced me to sign it." He still has the damn thing, he is pretty sure. It is in a box somewhere. And like a good soldier he did not talk for decades, not to nobody, not even his wife and kids.

Back in the states, Frank and Louie did get together—but instead of homemade ravioli they spooned food from a can. Louie's wife had sold every last piece of furniture, even the pots and pans. And soon he learned that she had been running around while he rotted in the camps. He started divorce proceedings and she left him for another man. Took the kids and everything.

Frank, not eligible for discharge, got assigned to a unit in Alabama training to fight the Japanese. Why did he sign that paper then? Not for this! He put up a stink, so they sent him to Camp Edwards on Cape Cod to guard conscientious objectors on work details. "I'm not going to hold a gun on Americans!" he shouted, and he managed a switch to supervising German POWs as they shingled roofs. But even then he stashed his gun, enough already, and just sat back and watched.

Louie and Frank kept company for a few years, but things just were not the same. Louie was different, out of gas, like he had left something in Germany. He skipped Frank's wedding and within a few years the men lost track of each other. It is hard to say why, exactly.

Frank got on with life, working long hours at the Post Office, sometimes gone from early morning to late at night—absent from home like his father, the pick-and-shovel man. He developed a drinking problem laced with

This is one of 20 panels in a quilt that Frank Molinari's daughter Paula made for him. Each panel contains an image from the "old days" or from her dad's wartime experiences. Here Louis Nigro (left) and Frank have a drink at the Valley Club. Louis saved Frank's life in the camps.

self-loathing, and he admits that sometimes he treated his wife and children abusively, until he sought treatment with the Veterans Administration in the 1980s. He cannot take his actions back, but he is sober now and guiding other ex-POWs to get help. Frank keeps a list of every ex-POW living in the state. Some have no one to care for them, he says. Some just refuse to come in from the cold.

The hurt goes very deep. Did the tough kid singing a cappella on street corners ever really exist?

Frank Molinari

Louie died several years ago. Frank did not learn about it until he was long buried. Hard to believe, that he went first. "I pray for that guy every day up in heaven," says Frank. Actually, Louie and Frank met one last time in the late 1970s, at Suffolk Downs race track. Frank finally told him the full story of what happened that awful day in the snowy woods. Louie replied, in a hard voice, that sometimes he wished he had died back there, that he had never made it home.

"Nobody gave a shit about us," said Louie. Frank looked at his angel and nodded. Then the two men watched the horses circle the track.

CHAPTER 9

What Is a Hero?

CROSSING OVER: CHESLEY RUSSELL'S STORY

Chesley Russell maneuvers with two canes to his kitchen table, rests his sore knees there, and rubs his arthritic neck. He no longer remembers his wartime experiences. Because those days are buried too deep for excavation, he cannot revise the chronology of events one more time or add a stray detail or subtract something that did not quite happen that way. From the cool remove of his 95 years, he is also denied the privilege of harkening back to his ancestor, John Roads Russell, who crossed the Delaware River with George Washington at his side. And that means everything for the proper telling of the tale.

"His memory's not as good as it used to be," kindly states his younger sister, Barbara Davies, who remembers the young Chesley as "a nice-looking man, always very active, enjoyed his family." As for his present fogginess, well, she says, "We're lucky it hasn't happened to us."

He must know he was a military man, though, because he still likes to be called Lieutenant Colonel—this according to his son, Richard Russell, a lawyer in New York City and a Vietnam veteran, born in 1942 just months before his father shipped off to England. After the war, Richard led a migratory childhood as his parents moved among Army posts in Japan, Germany, and the United States. Now when he writes to his father, Richard makes sure to inscribe "Lt. Colonel Chesley Russell" in big letters on the envelope.

Chesley Russell does not remember his experiences in World War II—at least not in the way that can be spoken—but he did write a short account two decades ago. It is 14-pages long, double spaced, and begins, "I was

Chesley Russell

captured off the coast of Normandy, France not far from Omaha Beach where I had landed with elements of my Combat Engr., Bn., the 121st Combat Engineers of the 29th Infantry Division. We were part of the initial land force on "D" Day, June 6th, 1944."

His "little craft," Chesley writes, perhaps with a measure of pride, "was the smallest of any vessel that crossed the channel under its own power."

Then he proceeds to record the boat's sinking by mortar fire as he disembarked. "I'm not sure whether all the men got off the ship but later I did see several of the crew trying to reach shore in a rubber raft." He takes note of the hundreds of dead bodies on the beach and the 50 percent casualty rate suffered by his battalion during the first two days. In the late afternoon of D-Day, we learn, his unit blew up a huge concrete obstacle that blocked the road leading away from the beach.

Most of their weapons and supplies, however, were destroyed or disabled by salt and sand. On the second day, within a maze of hedgerows that divided the landscape of Normandy, Chesley found himself the senior officer in a ditch full of men pinned down by machine-gun fire coming from every direction.

Was he being spared? A grenade landed beside him, but did not go off. A spent bullet hit him in the shoulder, but failed to penetrate his thick jacket. He was 35 years old, with three children back home; the soldiers around him were just kids, babies, and they were getting slaughtered one by one. Chesley could have escaped, he believed, crawled away like the commanding and executive officers had. Instead he took the responsibility of surrendering 60 men, a decision that does not appear to have plagued him. "I have never regretted what I did for the men," he writes.

But he did feel some bitterness at the C.O. and Exec. "They both got promoted and the C.O., a West Pointer, wound up his career as a Major General while I spent the rest of the war as a POW." Chesley performed their duty for them. He declares: "I decided that a good officer doesn't run away even if I didn't technically command those men."

These are the only sharp or judgmental words in his wartime document—he reserves none, even, for the Germans. The straight reportage, in fact, warms when Chesley's natural sympathies mix with resignation. An injured boy was taken away in a wagon. "We never saw him again," he writes. "I hope he got home OK eventually." Another time he watched a doctor remove gangrenous skin from an Allied soldier. "I hope he saved the boy's arm, but I've never seen him since."

The details come unadorned. Infested with ticks at a prison in Chalon-sur-Marne, his first destination as a POW, Chesley incurred "so many bites from head to foot that I could not recognize myself in the mirror." At Oflag 64, an officers' camp in Schubin, Poland, he calculated that POWs subsisted on 1,100–1,200 calories per day from the Germans (more likely, less than 1,000), plus Red Cross packages shared by several men at a time. Richard Russell remembers his father telling him about the awful potato soup, with bugs floating on top, and lousy turnips dug out of manure piles. (The stories were supposed to induce his son to finish his plate at dinner time, but usually produced the opposite effect.) Even as he starved, Chesley made himself walk every day around the inside perimeter of the barbed wire to maintain fitness.

Chesley Russell stands in a garden with his wife and son, Richard, circa 1952. The place is Kyoto, Japan, where Chesley was stationed. Richard Russell later fought in the Vietnam War.

Offlag 64, like some kind of mixed-up convention, was filled with "engineers, doctors, dentists, chaplains, actors, cobblers, tailors, businessmen." Chesley, eager to stay busy, took trigonometry and calculus lessons from the resident "math wizard" and called on his engineering degree from Tufts College (Class of 1931) to make a primitive pantograph that copied maps from a German newspaper to larger scale. He also designed a summer cottage—whether rustic retreat or pleasure palace, his document does not record—and he studied military law and helped dig tunnels that were never finished. They stashed the dirt in empty Red Cross boxes in the rafters. "Fortunately the framework above the ceiling was quite strong," states the engineer.

In December 1944, the Germans raided the barracks for uniforms and shoes, using them to dress up German spies infiltrating American lines during the Battle of the Bulge. Desperate to contribute to the war effort, the POWs gauged the distance and direction of missiles fired from a nearby V-2 buzz bomb site, and then encoded the information in letters home which, before reaching the hands of loved ones, were commonly read by Army intelligence. The prisoners imagined their words turning around to steer bombs to strategic targets—and so perhaps London would be spared and the war ended sooner. The helpless POW, a secret soldier.

There are many gaps in Chesley's story, events that are avoided or excused away. For instance, here is almost everything he writes about the hardships he endured in the winter of 1945, as men from his camp were marched west away from the Russian onslaught, as Hitler gathered his prisoners closer to the heart of the Reich:

> For the next three months our lives were put through a test of endurance both physically and mentally that as I think back was almost beyond comprehension. We walked through snow, blizzards, ice, rain, and of course some good days. We slept in hay barns at night and had very little to eat. To survive I learned to trade cigarettes for food, steal potatoes and vegetables and even bread and to keep walking even some days on my nerve alone. For the first 48 days I didn't take my clothes off once then I took a bath in a pig pen.

There is no self pity. He admits that they witnessed "of course some good days." The sun breaks out, even on a death march.

"Many incidents occurred during this trip which I don't have time to mention here," he writes, and we cannot help but wonder what postwar duties tore him from his desk. Perhaps his wife was calling. Perhaps the early deaths of two out of three children (one as a baby, one from an accident) made it hard for him to sustain focus on the past. Perhaps, in retirement after 25 years' service in the military, the part of him that wanted to forget was growing stronger, overcoming the part of him that felt it his duty to record the incidents.

Chesley Russell as a young soldier.

Many incidents occurred and "if you're interested," he extends the invitation, "I'll tell you about them sometime."

Absent his voice, another way to understand Chesley Russell is to draw a timeline from his small craft braving the English Channel in 1944 to John Roads Russell's low-riding wooden skiff in the dead of Christmas night, 1776. He and hundreds of Marblehead Marines shuttled about 2,600 soldiers across the Delaware River in a blinding snowstorm, their boats dodging ice knifing down the river. Once safely ashore, General Washington's troops surprised the Hessian mercenaries at Trenton and provided the Continental Army with its first resounding victory of the American Revolution.

Perhaps most importantly, the raid restored the new nation's morale—much in the same way the Normandy landings buoyed the spirits of the Allies. Only four American soldiers, incredibly, died in the battle at Trenton. Emmanuel Gottlieb Leutze's iconic painting in the Metropolitan Museum of Art, *Washington Crossing the Delaware,* is inaccurate in many details (for one thing, the boat sails a futuristic version of the American flag), but it captures the momentous power of the action, the sense of risk and daring. Leutze made a copy of the painting, actually, that was destroyed in an Allied bombing raid on Nazi Germany.

Two future presidents of the United States, James Madison and James Monroe, as well as Aaron Burr and Alexander Hamilton, crossed the Delaware that night, but they were not in the boat with General Washington. John Roads Russell was in that boat, a young private whipped by high winds and pulling water for all his life. He later rose to become Captain Russell and is buried on the grounds of the Unitarian Universalist Church in Marblehead, Massachusetts.

"We grew up hearing stories about John Roads Russell," says Barbara Davies, who points any doubters to a statue in front of the Trenton Battle Monument in New Jersey. There is a book about it, she says, but cannot recall the title. What is more, a great-great grandfather and a great-great uncle fought for the Union Army in the Civil War, one at the Siege of Vicksburg. Chesley was well aware of the family history, declares Barbara, and that tradition made a difference to him. But she balks at comparing John Roads Russell and her brother—after all, the Revolution and WW II were so different, were they not? Without a doubt, though, he took serving his country very seriously. Echoes Richard Russell: "That was his life, being a military officer."

In April 1945, after a 550-mile march, they were taken by train to a stalag in Moosburg bleeding with 30,000 POWs. Here Chesley's assessment seems detached, but not bitter: "We did have some people shot as prisoners in isolated incidents, but generally we were not beaten too much." Weeks later, army units under General Patton liberated the camp. "We were all very happy," Chesley writes, "when we saw an American flag go up at Camp headquarters."

That might seem a good image to cap a soldier's war story. The Stars and Stripes above, victorious, like the flag over Washington's head in a river-tossed boat rowed by John Roads Russell. The flag flying and the sweet dreams of home and family and freedom. But Chesley Russell, who died of old age in 2005, did not end his account there. For reasons of his own, forever irretrievable, he doubled back to the winter march that tested his will almost beyond comprehension. He left us, finally, with this: "One evening on our trip the guards had picked up a Russian who had escaped. He was

Chesley Russell

dying of starvation and exposure. Germans would not let our doctors care for him. The next morning I saw his body thrown on a manure pile."

WE WERE AMERICANS: HYMAN FINE'S STORY

"Hitler wanted all the POWs slaughtered," says Hyman Fine from the 18th floor of his apartment building in the Jamaica Plain neighborhood of Boston.

Hyman often sits on his balcony and looks westward across JP and West Roxbury and the bluish, suburban hills beyond. Jetliners bank in toward Logan Airport in the harbor, and sometimes the sight of a plane and the white contrail spreading apart in its wake will bring it all back for the 86-year-old man: running the gauntlet of flak and fighter planes across Europe in his B-24 Liberator; the bombers gathering wing tip to wing tip in a box over the target; the engines shot dead and burning on his 23rd and final mission, September 22, 1944; his bailout over the beautiful German countryside; and everything miserable after that.

Total liquidation of all prisoners, a directive straight from the Fuhrer. That was the rumor in Stalag Luft 1, a camp for airmen on the Baltic Sea,

Hyman Fine

winter of 1945. Why else had the SS taken control from the Luftwaffe? Why else had they cut rations to starvation levels and denied the POWs coal in the coldest weather to hit Europe in decades? And the hundred or so Jewish POWs segregated into two barracks, they would be killed first, of course.

"I knew Hitler was doing a job on the Jews," says Hyman, "but not how bad it really was." If the young navigator—at 24, old and wise for this war —could have risen over the wire and sailed just to the east, he would have looked down on the Bergen-Belsen concentration camp where at least 35,000 people died of brutal mistreatment, disease, and gruesome medical experimentation.

Hyman Fine was not moved to the Jewish ghetto at Stalag Luft 1. Why? Simply because the Nazis failed to catch on he was Jewish. That was it, and he wanted to keep it that way. When they had asked him his religion at the Oberusal interrogation center, "I just stood there mute," says Hyman, and for some reason they never looked at his dog tags, stamped with a big fat H for Hebrew. Back in the States, some Jewish soldiers had chosen A for atheist—or was it A for agnostic? Hyman's not sure.

"The guy who interrogated me spoke better English than I did," remembers Hyman, who followed the name, rank, and serial number routine but added the address of his wife in hopes the Germans would contact her. Six weeks earlier, Eve had given birth to their first child, Carl. That news had spurred him to fly even when he was sick—a towel wrapped around his neck, toilet paper in his back pocket—anything to make the mission limit and go home. Thirty-one got you sprung. Funny thing, Hyman was shot down on the day of his first wedding anniversary. Now he had a feeling he would not see his wife or kid for a long time.

As soon as he received his German POW dog tags (prisoner 5677), he hid his American tags beneath a board in his bunk. He remembers one airman back in England who collected hardware around his neck: Christian crucifixes, the Greek Orthodox cross of St. George, Turkish scimitars, the Jewish star, you name it. "I don't know which God will look over me," the man liked to say, "which one really exists—so what the hell, I'll wear them all."

What happened to that fellow, Hyman does not know, but he, too, believes that religions are not separate and exclusive. They have a lot in common. The Last Supper, he points out emphatically, was also a Passover supper. Jesus was a Jew.

In the late 1800s, his parents fled anti-Semitic attacks in Russia, into the west, and their son Hyman Fine was born in 1920 in the Roxbury section of Boston, in those days jammed with Italians, Irishmen, and Jews—all here due to hunger and persecution. "We got along, we didn't ask each other our religions," says Hyman. "We mixed, we mixed, we mixed." His father did well enough to own a little shoe factory and a house during the Depression, and he even gave his son a Buick when he enrolled at Boston University in 1938.

"I was a little wild," says Hyman, bopping with friends to every dance hall from here to Maine. When Pearl Harbor was attacked, in his senior year, he went to the draft board and received approval to finish his last semester, then arranged to join the Air Corps after graduation. "I didn't want to go into the Army and shoot people," he says. "Now dropping bombs, that was another story."

One night, in the back seat of a friend's car, Hyman found himself playing with the hair of a girl sitting in the front seat. It hung down for him, a waterfall of hair. She wore a tight white dress. They kibitzed and, well, "that was it," says Hyman, no matter that she went steady with another fella. No matter that she was the daughter of an orthodox rabbi and Hyman had a tendency to miss temple, to say the least. That was it, he says, so he hounded her. In August he got the call into the Air Corps and a month later Hyman married Eve.

He had wanted to wait, actually, but she said no. Eve told him, "Now or never." The world spun on the axis of now in 1942, so Hyman rode the rails

Hyman Fine as a young soldier.

back to Boston on his first furlough from flight training in Jackson, Mississippi. Eve wore her sister's wedding dress, good in a pinch, and Rabbi Abraham Rose married them in his temple. The newlyweds took a mini-honeymoon before he returned to duty, days late, and he was punished with full-pack "walk tours"—marching in circles, basically.

Soon Eve joined her husband at his next training stop in Florida. "You had to grab your happiness when you could get it," she says. She had never been to a restaurant, she was that green. Eve desperately wanted a baby, remembers Hyman, "In case I never came back." Now or never. For his part, "You don't think about being killed, just doing your duty and getting home." By the time his bomber group, the 491st, arrived in Greenland in June 1944, and then hopped to a base in England, he knew she was pregnant.

While he was overseas, Eve wrote Hyman a letter every day. He received only three of them as a POW, however, and one of those contained a photo of baby Carl. What was the chance of that? Hyman, though, does not recall or will not share what he felt when he first saw his son's face. "I'm not very demonstrative," he says, but also declares, "I showed it to everybody."

On July 25, 1944, Hyman's B-24, named *Pappy's Persuader,* participated in a strategic victory that was also a carnage of friendly fire. Operation Cobra, also known as the St. Lo breakout, enabled Allied troops to escape the Normandy peninsula and hurtle toward Paris. But the history books do not always mention that thousands of American infantrymen were killed, some vaporized to dust, by bombs dropped from their own planes. It was a simple screw-up: red smoke targeting Nazi troops blew back over Allied lines.

On that day Hyman remembers flying low at 5,000 feet, the flak from German antiaircraft guns so heavy that he was sure the plane would be shot down. The lead plane contained the master bomb site and the rest of the formation released their bombs only when the first plane let go. That was how it worked, you followed the leader. Operation Cobra was just his fifth mission. "After that," Hyman says, "nothing scared me."

He pulls out two photographs. One is his school portrait from Boston University, circa 1942, and in it he looks every bit the happy-go-lucky kid trolling dance halls and cruising in the Buick. Every bit the cad, playing with Eve's cascading hair as if he could gather her in by his fingertips. The second photo was taken in the summer of 1944 and shows Hyman receiving an air medal from General Kepner, after his tenth combat mission. He still looks like himself, but decades older and infinitely tired, and hollow. He stands rigid, as if he would collapse otherwise, and his eyes stare past the general who reaches to wrap another medal around another young man's neck.

A crowd of POWs stood at the camp fence and waved them in. It pleased Hyman immensely to be reunited with five men from his plane, including the co-pilot, Joe Cosgrove. They soon became "kriege brothers," sleeping in the same bunk and taking care of each other when they came down sick. Truth be told, until the SS takeover in January, life was not so awful at Stalag Luft 1. The men had chocolate bars and spam from Red Cross packages. There was a net for volleyball and the POWs played bridge and even had a small library. They gave each other haircuts to pass the time. Hyman grew a ridiculous mustache, curling it up with sealing wax scraped from parcels.

The POWs were allowed to roam between compounds. Once Hyman traded a cigarette holder Eve had given him for two cartons of cigarettes, on the theory that it was better to have the thing *now* than its container,

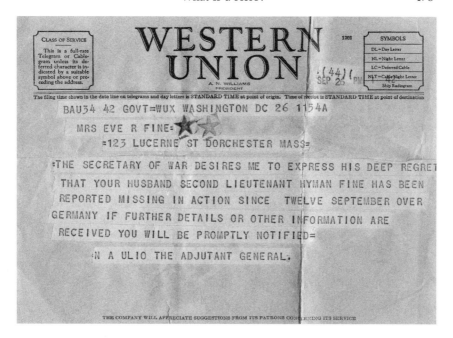

CLASS OF SERVICE

This is a full-rate Telegram or Cablegram unless its deferred character is indicated by a suitable symbol above or preceding the address.

WESTERN UNION

A. N. WILLIAMS
PRESIDENT

1201

SYMBOLS

DL=Day Letter
NL=Night Letter
LC=Deferred Cable
NLT=Cable Night Letter
Ship Radiogram

The filing time shown in the date line on telegrams and day letters is STANDARD TIME at point of origin. Time of receipt is STANDARD TIME at point of destination

BAU34 42 GOVT=WUX WASHINGTON DC 26 1154A

MRS EVE R FINE=

=123 LUCERNE ST DORCHESTER MASS=

=THE SECRETARY OF WAR DESIRES ME TO EXPRESS HIS DEEP REGRET
THAT YOUR HUSBAND SECOND LIEUTENANT HYMAN FINE HAS BEEN
REPORTED MISSING IN ACTION SINCE TWELVE SEPTEMBER OVER
GERMANY IF FURTHER DETAILS OR OTHER INFORMATION ARE
RECEIVED YOU WILL BE PROMPTLY NOTIFIED=

=N A ULIO THE ADJUTANT GENERAL.

THE COMPANY WILL APPRECIATE SUGGESTIONS FROM ITS PATRONS CONCERNING ITS SERVICE

Eve Fine received this telegram by hand on September 25, 1944. She knew it meant that her husband, Hyman, was either captured or dead. Thirty-five days later, another telegram informed Eve that he was a POW.

which only might hold something in the future. You played the odds. Eve would understand. He smoked all the cigarettes except for a few he gave to friends.

Sometimes, they even stood up to the Germans. Hyman remembers an American senior officer, Colonel Henry Russell Spicer, who defied the guards by ordering his men back to the barracks following hours of roll call on a cold November morning. After giving a "marvelous speech," Spicer was hauled away, court martialed by the Germans, and sentenced to six months solitary confinement to be followed by execution.

There was a great feeling of camaraderie among the POWs, asserts Hyman, even after the SS clamped down. He likes to think they would have rebelled if the Jewish POWs had been slaughtered. "We would have taken revenge," he says. "We were Americans."

But then, he admits, a riot might have gotten them killed, every last man in the camp. The SS were rough customers, all right, and they seemed to enjoy being cruel. Hyman avoided them like the plague. And they "starved us, absolutely starved us," he says. "We were so weak we could barely talk to each other." Between January and May 1945, his weight fell from 170 to 115 pounds. A collective shock set in among the POWs. "We just stood around like a bunch of dummies staring at each other." In March, at Bergen-Belsen 20 miles down the road, Anne Frank and her sister Margot died of typhus.

Russian troops liberated Stalag Luft 1 in the second week of May. A detachment from the American Air Corps arrived soon after. The SS guards had long fled, but some of them returned to camp in civilian clothes, believe it or not, asking to become prisoners of the Americans. They tossed the SS back out, says Hyman, for the Russians who "killed everything that moved."

Several weeks later, cruising into New York Harbor, Hyman cried when he saw the Statue of Liberty. All the men did. Eve waited at her sister's place in the City and she remembers watching through a window as the cab pulled up and her man got out and looked back at her through the glass. Hyman met his child—Carl was crawling by then—and soon he and Eve were living it up for ten days at the St. George Hotel in Atlantic City, on a special vets' rate of $1.20 a night. Then it was back to Boston and the normal American life they had never known, but had dreamed of, together.

"They didn't know, didn't understand what it meant to be a POW," says Hyman Fine. "We were looked down on like a bunch of cowards who gave up."

No one said the word coward to his face, exactly, but it was clear enough. Soon after his return he found himself getting angry easily. The nightmares started. His body ached. Eve and Hyman had two more children and one of them must have flushed both pairs of dog tags, German and American, down the toilet in a toddler prank. They looked everywhere, says Hyman, so the toilet was all they could figure. He took it hard losing those dog tags —just scraps of metal, sure, but somehow they meant a lot to him.

Of course, none of that was an excuse to belly ache. Lots of guys had it tough, Hyman knew that, just look at what Hitler did to the Jews. Think about what could have happened if he had not been on the right side of the war. Or if the rumors in the camp had come true, if the generals had carried out Hitler's desire to murder Allied POWs, Jews and all.

"I was in tough shape," says Hyman, "but I didn't realize it at the time."

He joined his father at the shoe factory and stayed there for the next 18 years. They made shoes for the Army and Navy and a good-looking, neoprene man's Oxford. When the Japanese took over the industry in the 1960s, Hyman became a traveling shoe salesman around New England. "Nothing lasts forever," he says. After the Japanese it was the Koreans making the shoes, and now the Chinese, and you pick who will do it next.

"All I know is shoes," he says. "I can still make a pair." It is almost as if he is waiting for an invitation to get up and prove it.

As for the war, Hyman wiped out the memories in an act of self-preservation—the daylight memories, at least. He simply tried his best not

Hyman Fine

to think about it. In the 1980s, most of the details began to rush back. Talking to other ex-POWs helped with the stress, their sympathy buoyed his spirits, but the nightmares still came. The planes banking toward Logan Airport still bring him back with a jolt, from his perch on the 18th floor.

Hyman says, "I'm all right now." He glances at his wife and she nods a little. "I've changed completely."

It is a funny thing, he adds, how attitudes about POWs have changed since the Persian Gulf War. That was the turning point, he believes. Those men came back after two weeks of captivity and were called heroes on TV. Hell of a thing. The president, God bless him, called them heroes, too. Then Hyman declares, shaking his head, sarcastic and grateful and amused all at the same time: "It took me 50 years to become a hero."

EPILOGUE

The scratchy voice on the other end of the line always startled me, the hollowed-out voice light as a feather, ever wary of the telephone con man, ever hopeful for the sound of a friend or loved one.

I would explain my purpose. Then, as if calling from another star system, I'd wait out the time lag, the silence broken by the static of thin wheezing. Their recognition was slow, but always enthusiastic. Yes, the guy about the POW book. That photographer, George, he said you'd call. Sure, I guess Saturday's good—and so commenced negotiations about the best time for my visit and, of course, the meticulous dispensation of directions.

Which way are you coming from? Do you know Route 3? Okay, there's an exit 20, 25 miles along next to the Shell station and you'll see a Dunkin' Donuts at the end of the ramp, on the right, but don't turn that way, that'll take you to Rhode Island, take a left and just keep going through five or six lights and you'll come out on a big rotary, follow it three quarters of the way around...

I scribbled garbled notes. In the end I would depend on MapQuest, but it seemed discourteous to interrupt an old man as he guided a young fellow from point A to point B, as he enjoyed the pleasure of being useful in a concrete way. Could a computer program warn of traffic swinging across lanes at Exit 17? Could it guide you back when you've gone too far?

Always their directions took me to the very end, to the driveway or parking spot, to the side porch door or lobby elevator, to their doorsteps. That's where I met each of them, 18 former POWs of Nazi Germany and one former POW of the Japanese Empire. On their doorsteps, hands outstretched, welcoming.

Jorg Meyer, my friend and colleague, photographed the men days or weeks before I arrived. His gentle manner warmed them up to speak and provided counterpoint to my intrusive questioning. To hear them testify to their pain could be an awkward experience, heightened by the incongruity of their cozy surroundings: the flowered couch pillows, the feminine knick-knackery on every surface, the photos of kids and grandkids wrapped around the walls like bandages.

Understandably, the men tried to steer the interviews to comfortable areas —success in combat, the elation of liberation, the first time they saw their bride—but they rarely refused to answer questions which they may have preferred to avoid. Men of the old school, they were always polite.

Fifteen of the men lived with their wives, two were widows, and two had never married. Sometimes the wife was not home during the interview or said a quick hello and receded to the bedroom. A few seemed downright hostile—who is this person, stirring up ghosts?—and one insisted that her man roll up the vacuum cleaner cord *like he'd promised* before he sat down with me.

Several stayed by their husbands' elbows, adding valuable commentary but mostly just being there, protectively, as their men told the old war stories retailored for male ears, for the permanence of pen on paper. Sometimes it felt, uneasily, as if I had become a safe conduit for the husband to tell the wife every last damn thing—so, finally, there it is.

How accurate are the memories of old men? How true are their memories of grim experiences 60 years old? Primo Levi, survivor of the Holocaust, examined the reliability of traumatic memories in his book *The Drowned and the Saved.* "Human memory is a marvelous but fallacious instrument," he wrote, and a terrible memory expressed in a story can become "crystallized, perfected, adorned, installing itself in place of the raw memory and growing at its expense." Unexpressed memories are vulnerable, too, he asserted, twisting of their own accord to protect the carrier or those he intends, one day, to tell.

His chronicle of Auschwitz, Levi believed, was "drenched in memory... thus it draws from a suspect source and must be protected against itself." Without equating POW captivity with the horror of the Holocaust, it is fair to say that *Journey Out of Darkness,* too, is drenched in memories that are, by their very nature, suspect to an unknowable degree.

Of course, I have consulted many books and internet sites to confirm basic facts of geography and chronology. But I have not, with a few exceptions, searched for corroborating accounts of specific events in the stalags. Such testimony, seen from different perspectives by different players, could be just as "crystallized, perfected" or morphed out of shape as the ones found here. Nonetheless, I believe this: every story in this book is real to the man who tells it, and I would be surprised if any of the men have consciously altered their accounts for selfish, or even selfless, reasons.

Driving home from our meetings, often shaken by the weight of sadness and shame that clung to these men, I questioned myself. How can I presume to understand the most wrenching experience of their lives, to connect with their enduring pain, from a series of interviews?

Ultimately, these essays are nothing more than encounters. I have bypassed the conventional first-person war story and instead taken core samples of each man—set pieces to be held up against Jorg Meyer's photographs which delve so deeply by presenting the surface of things.

I have also asked myself, what do I expect to gain from these men?

They are, I realize, roughly the age of my father if he had not died in 1975. Unlike these men, Harold LaCroix Jr. managed to avoid fighting and suffering in World War II, though just barely. A student at Harvard College in 1942, he joined the V-12 Navy College Training Program, as did 125,000 other college men. After years of training in tactical radar and sub chasing, he finally shipped out of Pearl Harbor on August 14, 1945—the day before Japan surrendered.

Thousands of men, including a few POWs in *Journey Out of Darkness*, had been yanked from V-12 or the Army Student Training Program and thrown into combat as "replacements" in 1944 and '45. For my lucky father, the Pacific War ended before it could kill him. And kill me, in a manner of speaking. If the A-bombs had fizzled and Allied troops had been forced to invade the Japanese mainland, my father may not have survived.

He was a gunnery officer on the destroyer escort *Joseph Auman*. Its mission was to deliver an underwater sea demolition (USD) team to a beach north of Tokyo. The boat, apparently, arrived in Tokyo Bay by September 2, in time for the signing of the peace treaty on the USS *Missouri*. According to the journal of a USD diver aboard the *Joseph Auman*, there was much tension between the ship's crew, deprived of their chance to serve in combat, and the battle-tested USD team. Cruising toward a finished war, my father may have felt an uneasy blend of relief and shame—a faint echo of the feelings that so many POWs experienced upon their liberation.

For nine months, the *Joseph Auman* shuttled cargo, mail, and passengers between China and the Philippines. It returned to San Diego in the summer of 1946 and was decommissioned, resurfacing as the *Tehuantepec* in the Mexican Navy. Harold LaCroix Jr. left active duty and became an insurance actuary in the suburbs of Connecticut. I was born 14 years later, the last of five children.

For ten days in mid-September 1945, however, the *Joseph Auman* docked in Yokohama Bay, and here extends a slim thread connecting father and son across time and space. Yokahama was a jumping-off point for thousands of surviving American POWs. Gabe Paiva, the ex-POW of the Japanese included in this book, went aboard an American ship there to start his journey home. It's probably a stretch, but maybe my father saw Gabe on the dock, gaunt and beaten down, or maybe he saw another man who had suffered as badly. Perhaps I have taken up the story that he glimpsed that day.

BIBLIOGRAPHY

Bradley, James. *Flags of Our Fathers*. New York: Bantam, 2000.

———. *Flyboys: A True Story of Courage*. New York: Little, Brown, 2003.

Cohen, Roger. *Soldiers and Slaves: American POWs Trapped by the Nazis' Final Gamble*. New York: Knopf, 2005.

Collins, Julia. *My Father's War*. New York: Four Walls Eight Windows, 2002.

Davis, Gawan. *Prisoners of the Japanese: POWs of World War II in the Pacific*. New York: William Morrow & Company, 1994.

Fussell, Paul. *The Boys' Crusade: The American Infantry in Northwestern Europe, 1944–1945*. New York: Modern Library, 2005.

Hacket Fischer, David. *Washington's Crossing*. New York: Oxford University Press, 2006.

Holmes, Linda Coetz. *Unjust Enrichment: How Japan's Companies Built Postwar Fortunes Using American POWs*. Mechanicsburg, PA: Stackpole Books, 2001.

Levi, Primo. *The Drowned and the Saved*. New York: Summit Books, 1988.

Nichol, John, and Tony Rennel. *The Last Escape: The Untold Story of Allied Prisoners of War in Europe, 1944–45*. New York: Viking Penguin, 2003.

O'Neill, William. *A Democracy at War: America's Fight at Home and Abroad in WW II*. Cambridge: Harvard University Press, 1998.

Skelton, William P., III. *The American ex-Prisoner of War, Lecture Series*. Washington, DC: U.S. Department of Veterans Affairs, 1999.

Spiller, Harry, ed. *Prisoners of Nazis: Accounts by American POWs in World War II*. Jefferson, NC: MacFarland & Company, 2004.

Taylor, Frederick. *Dresden: Tuesday, February 13, 1945*. New York: Harper Perennial, 2005.

Web sites:
www.axpow.org
www.census.gov
www.desausa.org
www.mansell.com
www.navsource.org/archives/
www.pegasusarchive.org/pow/stalag
www.va.gov
www.wartime-memories.fsnet.co.uk/pow (site now discontinued).
www.wikipedia.org

INDEX

ABOUT THE AUTHOR AND PHOTOGRAPHER

Hal LaCroix is a writer and college instructor who has taught for many years at Boston University. He has written for newspapers and magazines as well as environmental organizations including the Appalachian Mountain Club. LaCroix also has served as communications manager for the Immune Disease Institute at Harvard Medical School. He lives in Boston.

Jorg Meyer has photographed for clients including Fidelity, Stride Rite, the Immune Disease Institute, the Innocence Project, New York University, *The Boston Globe Magazine,* and *Italian Vogue Bambini.* His portraits of POWs were exhibited in 2006 at the National Heritage Museum. He divides his time between Boston and Charleston, South Carolina.

LYNNFIELD PUBLIC LIBRARY
LYNNFIELD, MASS. 01940